INSPIRATIONAL LANDSCAPE DESIGN IDEAS

THE artful GARDENER

GIL HANLY / ROSE THODEY

GODWIT

contents

❶ The pleasing form of this black pot by sculptor Rick Rudd is enhanced by the silvery green astelias growing behind it.

❷ Russell Fransham's subtropical garden at Matapouri Bay surrounds a reflective lake, creating an atmosphere of unrivalled tranquility.

introduction

Gardens are a unique art-form. They allow the gardener to explore his or her creativity using a living, growing, ever-changing medium. The key to a successful contemporary garden is the creation of a well-designed, low-maintenance outdoor living space, representing a refuge from the demands of modern life. In order to achieve this and to create an attractive outlook from the house or apartment at all times of the year, an artful approach is paramount.

Some gardeners and landscape designers are undoubtedly blessed with more artistic skill than others, and their gardens demonstrate how nature's raw materials can be transformed into startlingly beautiful environments. Sometimes this metamorphosis is achieved purely by innovative design and good gardening skills; sometimes by the clever selection and addition of works of art. In this book, we have tried to include some of the finest examples of art in the garden and the garden as art from New Zealand and around the world. In this way we can all learn from the skills and experience of the garden artists whose work is represented here. Some of the photos show private and public gardens that may be visited here, in Australia and south-east Asia, in North and South America, in Britain and Europe. The proliferation of outdoor sculpture exhibitions over the last decade is proof of the growing interest in this kind of art, whereas a fresh surge of interest in a more local art and crafts approach has also ensured a healthy quota of home-made or 'found' objects throughout the gardens.

Initially, a garden's impact depends on its visual appeal. From the moment we see it from the street, we get some idea of the unique style that has fashioned it. The owners may have used a variety of materials to separate it from the rest of the world; hedges,

An artistic approach can involve plants, chosen for their sculptural form or clipped to suit. Alternatively, we can decorate with hand-crafted objects and materials.

fences and walls of many different kinds. Everything, from the paths we walk on and the steps we climb, to the outdoor living spaces, in the form of balconies, decks, verandahs, courtyards, terraces, structures and finally the planting itself, stamps a particular pattern of texture, colour and form on the site, giving it its own individual character and allure.

Having laid the foundations, the artful gardener will then add specific features, ranging from the finest sculpture to antique urns and ornaments. Those with fewer means, but possibly greater imagination and talent, will turn simple containers and recycled bric-à-brac into all manner of interesting and decorative objects, from mosaic bird baths to rustic obelisks. Some get out the paintbrush, some stack pots or weave fences. Others clip, shape and train living green plants into hedges, espalier or topiary forms, or arrange those with inherently arresting and dramatic architectural or sculptural shapes into eye-catching patterns and groups. Still others are drawn irresistibly to water and

3 Designer Juan Grimm included exotic plants at the entrance to Papudo, on the central coast of Chile, while maintaining the existing native flora on the sea side of the contemporary house by architect Borja Huidobro.

❹ The depth of colour in Kevin Kilsby's brilliant blue mosaic water feature epitomises his skill at matching the intensity of his flamboyant subtropical garden with his art.

❺ Designed by Fiona Brockhoff to reflect its coastal setting, Karkalla, on the Mornington Peninsula, Victoria, is an eco-friendly garden, maintained without any irrigation. Native plants clipped into topiary forms sit well with the contemporary architecture of the house.

use it to add soothing sounds and images such as waterfalls, rills, fountains, fish ponds and glass-like reflective pools. Some will go so far as to paint vistas or create illusion with mirrors and false archways and doors to make small spaces appear larger or even limitless. At night, skilfully placed garden lighting can extend our pleasure in all of these features still further, adding a totally different dimension.

We hope this book will inspire both experienced and amateur gardeners to approach their property – whether it is large or small, in the heart of a city or deep in the countryside, old and established or new and freshly developed – with an artful eye, backed by plenty of enthusiasm and courage. With this in mind, we have arranged the text in a logical progression of chapters, taking you on a journey through the garden, from the entrance at the beginning, the walls that surround it, and the groundwork beneath your feet. Then we look at outdoor living spaces, sculpture, live plant material, the use of water, pots and structures before highlighting the possibilities of an earthy or rustic approach to decoration, and, finally, the magical effects of illusion.

Make the most of whatever is available: a can of paint can transform the old and ugly. A little experimentation can produce stunning results.

A garden presents us with an opportunity to create our own piece of paradise on earth. It is a slice of nature, not raw and untouched as we may find and appreciate it in the wild, but carefully moulded, nurtured and eventually transformed into an expression of our idea of natural beauty.

The ability to transform our vision into reality is the ultimate gift. We can all participate, have fun and enjoy the results of our efforts, whatever the scale. The secret lies in observation, confidence, wit and knowledge: we just have to learn to look, see, appreciate and then adapt for our own particular purpose. From a painted pot to a sculptural masterpiece, a little decoration and ornamentation in the right place is quite capable of converting your garden into a work of art. Rose Thodey and Gil Hanly

6 Pacific sculptor Tui Hobson turned the remaining trunks of three gum trees – that had to be cut down on Nora West's property in Ponsonby – into eye-catching works of art.

7 Retro basket-weave bucket chairs frame a path decorated with skeleton figures that leads to a cheery, colourful sleepout at Matt Wilson's Wellington home.

8 Designed by glass artist James McMurtrie, with landscape designer John Middleton, for the Melbourne International Flower and Garden Show, 2006, this giant 'water spout' is a spectacularly intricate and complex sculptural work.

The entrance to your home reveals a lot about you. Does yours say what you want it to? Take a fresh look and see what an artistic approach might achieve.

1. Fern gates.

2. Reed gate.

❶ (Previous page) Landscape designer Mark Read has created a masterpiece with these magnificent gates, fusing motifs from the industrial revolution and Victorian England with Kiwi fern patterns into a seamless blend. The ferns and the navigational globe on top are painted a bronze-grey colour with a special mix of metal oxide paint.

❷ The vertical raupo design on this gate relates to the wetlands setting of this property, while the palm fronds indicate a modern dwelling. It proves that safety requirements for swimming pools need not be a barrier to artistic design.

❸ The use of paua shell and glass-fibre-reinforced polyester material places this unique gate squarely in a South Pacific context and allows a tantalising glimpse of the courtyard beyond.

❹ Twizel blacksmith Noel Gregg designed this wrought iron gate decorated with a duck and supporting plants to complement the native planting at the Avon River entrance to this Christchurch property.

3. Paua gate.

4. Duck gate.

What does your entrance say about you?

Arriving at someone's house is always tinged with a sense of heightened expectation. Even if they are old friends and you have visited a thousand times before, there is still that feeling of being granted permission to enter, of being admitted to someone else's private zone.

Coming home should fill you with a warm sense of familiarity and pleasurable escape into your own personal realm as soon as you shut the gate or door on the world outside. Putting in some effort to make sure that your homecoming will always have this effect is the first step towards creating your own unique space. When you claim an area, you are merely following your instincts to protect yourself and provide a shelter from the vagaries of existence. This is how you define yourself, how you establish your boundaries and then invite others into your private domain. Be bold; be passionate – throw yourself into the fray. Make certain that this important stamp of individuality is a genuine reflection of you and your

5 Designed by William Kent in the eighteenth century, the gardens at Rousham House, Oxfordshire, remain relatively untouched. Gates like this arched one in the walled garden entice visitors to explore further.

6 By repeating the pattern of the intricate fretwork on the restored colonial villa, these black steel gates set in a solid stone wall reinforce the impressive attention to detail of a bygone era.

7 This modern interpretation of a pair of traditional wrought iron gates uses a bold V-shape at the top to add interest to the vertical lines, and to echo the triangle and diamond pattern at the bottom.

8 The unadorned vertical bars in this modern steel gate match the formal precision of the garden, as reflected in the row of immaculate bay standards underplanted with balls of box and mondo grass.

innate sense of creativity, because anybody who approaches a house and garden forms an immediate impression. From large and imposing residences to small and cosy cottages, a window is opened on to the kind of people who might live there.

Personalities will be reflected in every detail: the gate, the walls and paths or lack of them, the type and style of planting. Are these people friendly and welcoming? Do they have a sense of humour? Is their privacy obviously of paramount importance? Perhaps security is clearly an issue in how they present themselves to the world.

Whatever your requirements, it is important to begin with the style of the house in deciding how your entranceway should look. To make a pleasing impression the whole image must be in harmony. A white picket fence belongs to an earlier era of highly decorative architecture, whereas a modern building will require clean lines and sharper definition.

Contemporary gardens approach the need for enclosure by drawing inspiration from many different countries and cultures around the globe. Form and texture, reinforced by the use of colour, are fundamental to the establishment of mood and atmosphere. Such gardens are often brave and not

5. Blue gate.	**6.** Fretwork gate.	**7.** V-shaped gates.

8. Iron gate.

11. Flower gate.

9. French farmhouse.

10. Freestyle design.

9 A richly ornate wrought iron gate conjures up the French tradition of lavishly embellished entrances, while the plain ochre tones of the farmhouse-style building provide a perfect foil.

10 A beautifully understated design of horizontal curved lines adds a flourish and breaks the monotony of vertical iron bars. It stands out clearly against the white stone steps.

11 Painted a rich terracotta to match the abstract mosaic pattern on the terrace, this floral wrought iron gate, designed by Noel Gregg, makes a strong artistic statement.

12 When the solid street gate is open this entrance reveals a welcoming archway of copper beech framing a fine iron gate which allows a view through to the house.

13 The roadside gate at the same property provides a solid impenetrable barrier, softened by detailed ironwork which repeats the pattern of the wrought iron gate inside.

always entirely successful, but each dramatic leap into the unknown will result in at least a small step towards the development of a new and improved underlying standard. Bits of these designs will endure and ultimately become a classic part of garden design and then we will look back and see that progress was made.

Even if you lean more to the reassuring formality of symmetry or the relaxed informality of a rambling, natural look, it helps to be aware that the new materials available today can give these approaches a clever new twist, a fresh emphasis that will revitalise and energise your garden provided you are prepared to experiment a little. Gardens are the most malleable of creations, so keep an open mind and see what evolves.

Before you get carried away, though, it will pay to start by checking with your local council to see what its requirements are. Restrictions apply to the height and type of most major structures you might want to erect, beginning with fences and walls. It may even be necessary to have the site surveyed to make sure the boundary line you've taken for granted is accurate.

12. Layered entrance.	**13.** Solid gate.

14 The owner found these ancient gates in an antique shop in Central Otago. Such is the simplicity of their classic lines, they complement the modern architectural features of the property beautifully.

15 Landscape designer Trudy Crerar's artistic eye is evident in this perfectly proportioned entrance, where the fine lines of the metal gate allow a view through to the well-maintained hedging and conifer spirals.

16 Such an attractively roofed doorway deserves a finely balanced gateway to match: clipped hedges and wall plants complete the perfect picture.

17 Purpose-built seats at the entrance to this house in Melbourne, Australia, mean that the owners can sit down and pass the time of day with neighbours wandering by.

Tall fences and walls create an obvious barrier and deflect intruders at the outset. More discreet screening can be achieved by planting taller shrubs and trees at strategic points inside the boundary. With gated communities at one end of the spectrum and open North American front gardens at the other, there is plenty of scope for your own individual imprint, made according to your particular needs and preferences.

A simple approach to organising your entrance and, in fact, your whole garden is to examine the way you like to live. Do you prefer an orderly, planned existence, or does a more relaxed lifestyle suit you better? Do you aspire to the myth of maintenance-free properties or are you a maniacal workaholic? Are children and family pets part of the equation, or is this a pet-free, adult habitat? Do you lean more towards the plant collector brigade or are you a design addict?

Once you have jotted down some of these home truths, your preferred style – formal or informal, relaxed and casual, weird and whacky, pared-back minimalism or cheerful clutter, antique, retro or contemporary – will quickly become obvious. You may already have worked out where you fit, from

14. Egyptian gates.	**15.** Formal topiary.	**16.** Roofed entrance.

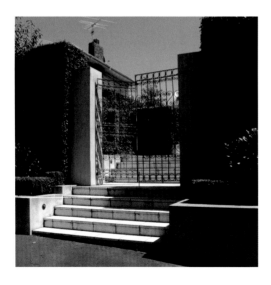

17. Seated entrance.

18 Shiny three-dimensional stainless steel bars in vertical box sections match the restrained minimalism and horizontal lines of the house. At night, subtle downlighting picks out the pots and clearly delineates the main entrance.

19 Black-coated wooden bars correspond to the fence and give this gateway a clean-lined, unified look. As a practical solution to the steeply sloping section, the gate slides back instead of swinging open.

20 These woven metal gates open up to reveal this abstract aluminium sculpture by Marté Szirmay and are in keeping with the materials used in the garden.

21 A solid basket-weave pattern at the base of vertical iron bars adds solidity and a degree of privacy to this gate, which is balanced by the contrasting texture of the stone pillar.

22 Horizontal bars at the top of this domestic entrance soften the impact of heavily textured woven metal normally reserved for industrial use.

building or decorating your house. The exercise then becomes one of establishing a sense of continuity – tying the entrance garden to the house in the smoothest possible way.

By matching the materials, colours and textures of perimeter walls, fences and gates with those used in the house itself you will achieve the required blend. If both house and gate are wooden, for example, you can match the paint colour or stain used on the front door with that of the gate. Fretwork trimming a colonial villa or bungalow can be echoed in the detailing of an iron or wooden gate.

Rock, brick, concrete and wood are solid, long-lasting materials that can be used on their own with most types of house. Combinations such as iron and steel with wood or concrete usually work better with modern houses, while older styles of architecture can be enhanced by composite fences of stone or brick topped with iron railings between solid pillars.

18. Stainless steel gates.	**19.** Horizontal bars.

22. Industrial metal.

20. Woven metal gates.

21. Combination gate.

23. Japanese gate.

㉓ This solid wooden construction at the entrance to a home on Sydney's North Shore portrays Japanese influences, with its intricate patterns and fine sense of balance.

㉔ Contrasting materials are cleverly combined in an interesting blend of colours and textures to make this inviting entrance above a water feature in this Melbourne home.

㉕ The external walls are painted a contrasting colour to those inside, adding to the sense of entering a safe, soothing haven, in this low-allergy garden designed by Xanthe White.

Access to contemporary homes is often by wide, generous, floating concrete steps rising to solid, imposing and impenetrable front doors, negating the need for a barrier from the street. Minimalist planting will be all that is required in support, but a visitor's curiosity will be piqued as to what type of house and back garden lies well hidden behind that serious door.

A solid wall or thick, dense hedge is capable of reducing the amount of traffic noise you have to endure in your front garden. Such a barrier will also add to your garden's sense of privacy in that passersby will not be able to eavesdrop so readily on your outdoor conversations. For extra insulation, cover solid walls with climbing plants, as these will dampen the sound still further.

Practicality should be given equal weight to other considerations in all your decisions. Is it easy to see the number of your house from the street? If visitors arrive at night will they be able to find the keypad or latch in the dark? Adequate but unobtrusive lighting is needed in these areas, along with clear markers

24. Floating entrance.	**25.** Walled entrance.

26 Landscape designer Trudy Crerar has left this town-house entrance garden open to the street so that passersby can share in the beauty of its contrasting foliage.

27 The entrance to Chilean landscape architect Juan Grimm's own garden demonstrates his preference for using native flora to create natural-looking gardens that sit well within the wider landscape.

28 Isabelle Greene designed the garden of this home in Santa Barbara, California, where curving red handrails and a supporting pole extend a warm welcome to visitors.

as to where the front door is. You probably don't want the courier or meter reader wandering around to the back of the house when you are reclining by the pool. For the visitor, nothing is more disconcerting than arriving at a property and wondering which ranch slider is the appropriate one to knock on.

Structures in a garden provide a wonderful opportunity for artistic expression, and gates are the ultimate entrance. Simple, rustic forms portray an earthy, naturalistic approach, while large iron structures suggest formality. Whatever you choose, the scale must be in proportion to the architecture of the house to present a balanced, aesthetically pleasing impression. Sometimes it is useful, as well as attractive, to have an open gate with bars or spaces so that you can see who is coming to the house and passersby can get a tantalising glimpse of the front garden and house within.

Why not design your own gate and have it made up by a skilled craftsperson in wood, iron or

26. Open entrance.	27. Grimm's garden.

28. Curved entrance.

29. Papudo, Chile.

29 Designed by Juan Grimm, these broad, floating steps meander through the foliage of densely planted ground-cover to create a pleasing entrance to a coastal property in Chile.

30 Reinforced steel and concrete have been used to foil vandals in this handsomely striped letterbox on a busy street. Pots of zinnias match the terracotta tiles to perfection.

31 Floating steps flanked by silver birch trees (*Betula utilis* var. *jacquemontii*) and mondo grass combine in a tableau of simplicity. The Roman numeral stencilled into a sheet of copper makes a distinctive letterbox.

galvanised steel? Swirls delineating waves or shells; the outlines of flowers, leaves, seed pods or branches; combinations of circles, stars, teardrops, geometric shapes or purely abstract concoctions can be extremely satisfying to call your own. Is there a family symbol that can be pressed into use? What about a favourite animal, fish or bird incorporated into the surface? A random or themed collection of found objects, perhaps? Or some serious minimalism in the form of vertical, horizontal or daringly diagonal steel aluminium or wooden rods?

Alternatively, it can be fun to create a sense of mystery with a solid gate that you have to open to see what is behind it. Then the whole scene is not revealed all at once but is discovered layer upon layer, once you step inside.

Where space is severely limited, or the entrance is on sloping ground, a sliding gate or door is often a practical solution to prevent the gate hitting the ground when it is opened. In this case, you can hide the

30. Striped letterbox.	**31.** Street entrance.

32. Rustic gate.

33. Leaf gate.

34. Moon gate.

35. Floral gate.

36. Walled gate.

32 A rusty iron gate leading to a side entrance lends a suitably weathered air to the post and rail fence on this rural property at Waimauku, near Auckland.

33 A pattern of swirling leaves on an arched iron gate sets the scene at the entrance to a verdant garden.

34 A circular moon gate set in a contrasting pattern of square trellis offers a view through to the garden.

35 A fanciful floral gate made out of corrugated iron by sculptor Jeff Thomson provides an attractive screen for the owners' compost bins at the end of a garden path.

36 A solid, impenetrable barrier need not be harsh and unappealing, as this gate, designed by Thomas Hobbs and set in a contoured terracotta wall in Vancouver, British Columbia, amply demonstrates.

37 Designed by Maureen Busby, this gold medal-winning garden at the Chelsea Flower Show, 2004, illustrates *shizen* – the Japanese ideal of perfect harmony between house, garden and surroundings.

gate altogether by making it from exactly the same materials as the fence or wall to create a unified look. Horizontal metal bars or wooden slats can look extremely sleek and smart in the appropriate setting. Sheets of industrial metal are another possibility.

Once inside the gate, clear markers as to the direction you need to go to find the front door can take all kinds of forms. Planting a low hedge beside a paved path leaves no room for doubt, but other, more subtle markers can be effective too. Large containers placed at strategic points work well, as do paired plants on either side of the walkway. To make a small space appear larger, it is often better to treat it as an entrance courtyard, rather than splitting it in two with a path up the middle. Circular, oval or asymmetric shapes defining the space can be effective, so long as the front door is obvious, and they can either be paved to provide a hard-wearing surface or treated with a porous material like fine gravel,

37. *Shizen* — the Japanese way.

38 A simple wooden gate introduces variations on the blue theme used to reflect the sparkling sea below this modern house set above the Waitemata Harbour.

39 A modern interpretation of a handsome roofed or covered gateway like those found at the entrance to a churchyard. Clipped teucrium defines the roadside planting.

40 The humble picket fence can be reinterpreted to complement grander homes by simply raising the pillars to make them more imposing and placing solid ball caps on top for extra height.

pebbles or crushed shell to allow water to soak back into the ground.

Your front door should be sheltered from the weather by an overhanging roof of some kind, in keeping with the architecture, so that visitors are protected from the rain. You won't want, either, to be left groping for your keys while the shopping bags and the drycleaning – to say nothing of the baby and the toddler – get a thorough soaking. The steps or paving up to the front door should be as generous as possible, clearly delineating the area as the main entrance. To make it more welcoming, add a sculpture, or a decent-sized container or two, but make sure they are firmly anchored if the door is accessible to the street.

Even in the pokiest of urban dwellings, you can make an entrance more inviting by brightening the colour scheme of hard surfaces, pots and containers to make it look more cheerful. Remember though, that you are part of a neighbourhood and, unless you can make a bold artistic statement successfully, it might be wiser to blend gracefully instead of striking a discordant note. That said, something truly

38. Blue gate. | **39.** Lych gate.

40. Victorian gate.

41. Boat arch.

41 Artist Dick Frizzell dreamt up this iconic watery archway, complete with fish, wine goblets and wooden boat bobbing about on the waves at the top.

42 Bright, bold sunflower-yellow topped off with vivid sky-blue trimmings should be enough to lift the spirits of anyone passing by this house.

43 Manuka battens combined with a wrought iron gate painted bright blue make for a warm and wacky welcome at landscape architect Rebecca Wilson's former home in Eastbourne, Wellington.

original can be uplifting and liberating, even becoming an icon or a landmark.

Perhaps you've always hankered after a moat? Why not? Gliding to the door over water will guarantee that life is never dull at your house. Concrete steps or steel planks, with the odd stepping stone, will appear to float on the surface, making the atmosphere somewhat surreal, especially when lit at night.

Cars can kill a beautiful entrance dead. If they have to be accommodated at the front, it can become a major challenge to prevent them becoming too dominant. If they can't be dealt with discreetly to one side and effectively hidden, you will have to rely on a clever layout and even more inspired planting. Instead of laying an enormous expanse of dull concrete, work out the exact movement and space required for entering and exiting, including a turning bay if there is space. Then add beds of evergreen shrubs to soften the overall effect. Instead of a sea of grey, the offending garage will be just visible

42. Sunny entrance.	**43.** Eclectic mix.

44. Rustic circles.

45. Urban design.

46. Twisted metal.

44 Found objects on a circular theme decorate a gate designed by potter and sculptor Tim Holman in the Coromandel.

45 Everyday metal objects in many guises are successfully melded together to make a sharply eye-catching statement at an entrance in Newtown, Wellington.

46 A twisted black metal gate designed by Dave Vazey reinforces the rustic elements of river stones and weathered wooden posts that frame the entrance to a home in Glendowie, Auckland.

47 Stone arches by sculptor Chris Booth enclose a fine pebble archway to form an impressive entrance at Takahanga Marae, Kaikoura.

beyond a soothing screen of plants. If there is room for a traditional turning circle, you can even consider mounding the sides of the driveway before planting. Depending on the height of the mature plants, this will help keep the house partially hidden from view until you arrive in front of it.

Disposing neatly of household rubbish is imperative. Don't let unsightly bins and recycling containers blur that sense of perfection you have achieved. With a minimum of extra effort you can hide them in a convenient spot behind a simple horizontal or vertical trellis cage, for example; either painted to match the fence, wall or gate, or left to age naturally to a pleasing silvery grey colour. If a patch of earth is available, add a small, well-behaved climbing plant for that final touch of concealment.

Having successfully designed the cover of your book, you can now step confidently inside and continue the narrative or journey by building upon the elements that will make your garden a uniquely inviting, pleasantly amusing and utterly intriguing place – and inevitably a clear reflection of you and your personal story.

47. Takahanga marae.

They surround and cocoon us from the outside world. Being vertical, they also hit us in the eye, presenting an unrivalled canvas for artistic expression. Don't let this opportunity pass.

1. Stone wall.

1 (Previous page) Delicate ferns add a soft touch of green to this beautifully constructed stone wall at the entrance to Ibah Hotel on the banks of the Oos River in Ubud, Bali.

2 A series of louvred screens gives a sense of privacy without the dominating block effect of a solid wall. Planting breaks up the line still further.

3 This artistic compilation of piled rocks and desert planting is set off to perfection by the skillful combination of materials and use of colour in the wall behind.

4 A series of curved walls in aged, rusty-looking Cor-Ten steel defines the xeriscape planting in the succulent garden of Sydney's Royal Botanic Gardens.

The vertical dimension in any garden presents a creative opportunity par excellence. This is where you look from the house, before your eye is caught by other elements such as the ground and what has been used to cover it. As the gardener and property owner, you have the immediate view entirely in your hands, and the range of options is vast.

A boundary fence or wall frames the garden and makes us feel enveloped and secure in something that is of a manageable, human scale. While we might adore the great outdoors and the wildernesses of the world, we don't necessarily want to live in them. We want to feel safe, sheltered and protected from unwanted views of ugly buildings, backyards, alien skyscrapers and other people's animals, cars, motorbikes and skateboards. Apart from protecting our boundaries, we often need internal divisions for

2. Louvred screens.

3. Walled desert.

4. Cor-Ten steel.

5. Woven wall.

5 Sydney-based designer Richard Unsworth of Garden Life has incorporated a woven hanging and adjacent water feature to add texture and decorative interest to this solid concrete wall.

6 Designer Susan Firth has used 'baby' corrugated iron to confine this inner-city garden, giving it a more refined, urban look.

7 Instead of succumbing to the perceived notion of the pool fence as an essential but ugly blot on the landscape, this version by landscape architect Vladimir Sitta ably succeeds in enhancing the handsome architectural features of this Sydney home.

safety around swimming pools and to divide or screen different areas of the garden. These are important structural decisions and you have to decide what will work best for you and how much maintenance you are prepared to do. Should you build a solid wall of brick, stone or concrete? These materials are often available from local sources and the colour will then blend in with neighbouring houses in the larger landscape. Do you want to enhance the richly textured surfaces or would a sleek, smooth finish be a better match for your home?

Perhaps a wooden fence would suit your purposes better. Timber can be used in an endless variety of ways – separated to allow tiny gaps for light and air and brief glimpses of and from passersby, or solid and completely private. You might want to combine a solid base with an open pattern of trellis at the top to lighten the look. Then again, a rustic, organic fence of driftwood or a woven material such as willow, brush or bamboo might be the answer.

Picket fences have a certain charm that is part of our inheritance. You don't have to slavishly adhere to the original white variety, however: paint them to match your house or some other aspect of the property. The detail can be varied too – plain rounded ends are available, as are square-cut ones.

6. Corrugated iron.

7. Pool fence.

8 The soft layer of moss and ferns covering this stone wall at the Ibah Hotel in Ubud, Bali, adds to the special atmosphere found only in the damp heat of the tropics.

9 Colourful violas in terracotta pots stand out against the mixture of evergreen and deciduous foliage used to cover a plain brick wall in an Auckland garden.

10 A climbing plant such as this Boston ivy (*Parthenocissus tricuspidata*) transforms a blank wall in a small city courtyard into a living garden, with cool green effects in spring and summer, followed by autumn colour and then winter tracery.

11 The winter-flowering orange trumpet vine (*Pyrostegia venusta*) is the perfect choice to display against the natural wood and dark brown tones of a Sydney wall.

Sometimes you see such fences combining in narrow uprights with wider ones and painted different colours. It doesn't always work, but it can.

Traditional wrought iron has metamorphosed into an infinite array of practical options, from basic swimming pool fences to elegant chic simplicity in galvanised steel or aluminium. Metal pickets on top of stone or brick will look less imposing than a solid wall but will still be impenetrable. Cheaper options such as corrugated iron can be both effective and smart if painted and framed or finished in a way that is compatible with the house. You might want to design your own metal fence or use railings found at a demolition or recycling yard. Don't hesitate to approach a blacksmith or iron worker as they may enjoy the chance to use a bit of creativity and suggest things you hadn't thought of, all for a surprisingly reasonable price.

Cor-Ten steel panels are increasingly popular, as they have been treated to look prematurely rusty or aged, giving the garden a distinctly earthy backdrop. Highly versatile, the panels can be cut to add another dimension along the top, or a pattern can even be stencilled into the material like a frieze. Try a circular motif cut at random and repeat it on the ground plane with tiles or round pavers and furnishings.

8. Balinese wall.

9. Wall-mounted pots.

10. Green wall.

11. Matching climber.

12. Star jasmine wall.

12 The strong grid pattern of star jasmine (*Trachelospermum jasminoides*) on the wall of this house in Alfriston, Auckland, adds a touch of restful green, and a pleasant perfume, while breaking up the wall's large expanse.

13 Fine wooden runners add definition to a plain concrete wall, generously planted with Boston ivy for year-round variety.

14 A combination of stone and concrete in a layered arrangement provides an effective solution to a retaining problem. Dry-tolerant plants thrive in the heat generated by the hard surfaces.

Gabions – baskets or mesh cages filled with stones – have long been used as effective retaining walls. Nowadays they have moved into the forefront of landscaping as they give a natural yet contemporary edge to the design. A combination of timber and gabions in the right proportions can provide a physically strong wall that still manages to look harmonious in a natural setting. Open post and rail arrangements have a handsome country air and are well suited to the roadside boundaries of lifestyle blocks and farms where large animals graze.

For divisions within the garden itself, screens are the answer. They will provide a sense of mystery just by indicating that part of the scene is hidden, which also makes the garden feel bigger than it actually is. They are obviously practical too, as they will protect you from being seen by the neighbours, should you want some outdoor privacy to sit and read, sunbathe, or relax in the spa pool. They don't have to be enormous: a low wall is all you need if you are going to be sitting behind it in a lounger.

A screen can be made of aluminium or painted wooden louvres, bamboo, trellis, lines of stakes placed closely together, brush, woven material, or even that opaque synthetic material used in interior

13. Boston ivy wall.	**14.** Retaining wall.

⑮ By mixing contrasting foliage and fence materials, designer Vladimir Sitta has created a tapestry of patterns and textures in this Sydney entrance.

⑯ By limbing plants up to expose the trunks, and merging the canopy of branches at the top, the base of this wall is left free for further decoration and planting.

⑰ At Hidcote Manor Garden in the Cotswolds, parallel pleached hedges illustrate the different effects to be gained with different backdrops.

⑱ Formal clipped topiary forms give a firm sense of structure in this Wellington garden designed by Kim Jarrett. Flowing native plants such as (*Chionochloa flavicans*) are like the soft strokes of a paint brush.

bathroom panels. If these look a bit stark, decorate them or cut out stencilled patterns to make them more attractive.

Sometimes you can be faced with three different fences or walls belonging to neighbouring properties on all sides. Occasionally, just one will be enough to put you off your coffee. What you do on your side is your business, so if you want to get a more uniform or agreeable look, cover the walls with a single material of your choosing. It doesn't have to be expensive and you don't have to aim for a complete cover. Get creative and make a Japanese or oriental-style camouflage with bamboo or fine battens attached to the existing walls in a simple latticework pattern.

Hedges are the living alternative to a constructed barrier but will need regular clipping and shaping to be effective, and may take years to establish. In a tiny garden, they can take up too much of the available space – much more than a flat wall or fence. By using trees that grow naturally in a vertical and dense manner, such as some of the conifers, you can reduce the need for constant trimming. To get the best of both worlds, add plants to walls and fences, either by using climbers to cover them, or by growing

15. Foliage effects.

16. Pleached elms.

17. Hedges on stilts.

18. Topiary mix.

19. Stone scroll.

19 Set in antique dealer Michael Trapp's woodland garden in Connecticut, this classical stone scroll on top of a loosely piled stone wall gives the area a unique focus.

20 Rebecca Wilson designed this driftwood wall to reflect the warm light of the setting sun for a house by the sea in Eastbourne, Wellington.

21 Gabions filled with large river stones make compact striking pillars and support this board fence outside a property on the road to Taylor's Mistake, near Sumner, Christchurch.

22 Tree stumps made of scorched and untreated oak by sculptor Walter Bailey create a visual barrier in the Hannah Peschar Sculpture Garden in Ockley, Surrey.

20. Driftwood wall.

21. Bamboo rock.

22. Journey Work.

23. Swings.

23 This stone gabion pavilion garden of swings from the Chaumont-sur-Loire Garden Festival, 2006, was designed as a place to escape from the troubles of the world and relish the memories of childhood.

24 Christchurch landscape architect Jeremy Head designed this massive bridge-beam timber frame and gate, flanked by mesh windows allowing views through to an internal courtyard.

25 Cut-out walls abound in this garden of silhouettes, reflections and illusions, designed to simulate the imagination of children playing hide and seek.

taller specimens at strategic points, with massed groups inside the perimeter. Be aware of the borrowed landscape of neighbours' trees beyond the walls as they can also enhance your outlook.

Hedges can be shaped or pleached so that their trunks are limbed up or stripped of branches and then the tops are trained to grow together, creating a visual barrier at a certain height. If required, a solid fence can be built behind the clean line of trunks to make the area completely private.

Yew is planted extensively in the northern hemisphere to create solid, tall hedges. Here you can substitute Podocarpus totara (totara). Coprosma repens (taupata) is another native possibility, along with Corokia x virgata 'Cheesemanii' and Pittosporum crassifolium (karo). For a lighter-screening, grey-green effect, try Olearia lineata (a native tree daisy) or olive trees. Larger-leafed green options include Griselinia littoralis (broadleaf) 'Whenuapai' or the lighter green 'Broadway Mint'. For smaller growing hedges within the garden, try Coprosma 'Middlemore', Corokia x virgata 'Silver Ghost,' and Myrsine divaricata (weeping matipo) 'Poor Knights', or the several varieties of buxus (box) now available.

Some climbers quickly become thugs and you may well wish you'd never thought of them. Evergreen

24. Timber and mesh.

25. Imaginary garden.

26 Burlap sacks represent battlefield trenches in this playground garden from the Chaumont-sur-Loire Garden Festival, 2006. Planted with round boxwoods, the walls enclose a room designed like a fortress.

27 The smooth-flowing effect of this gently curving wall in the Chinese Garden of Friendship, Darling Harbour, Sydney, supports a prevailing sense of balance and harmony.

28 Pliable metal threaded through the horizontal dowel bars of these tall screens provides ribbon-like decoration and block just enough of the view to entice you to wander further through the garden. The colours match the mixed planting for added effect.

ivy, for example, can spread way beyond your perceived limits and will leave unsightly marks if you try to get rid of it. Some climbing figs are also difficult to control unless kept firmly within bounds. Deciduous Boston ivy (*Parthenocissus tricuspidata*), on the other hand, is easily removed and the tracery looks attractive even in the depths of winter when its scarlet autumn leaves have long gone.

Plants like bougainvillea can provide a wonderful splash of contrasting colour to a plain wall in a warm climate and a single plant may be all that is needed. It won't need pampering, either; instead it thrives on neglect. A simple way to fill your whole garden with perfume is to cover a wall or trellis in star jasmine. You can add to the decorative effect by growing it in a diamond, square or rectangular pattern along wires and it will need only one good cut back a year.

You may want security and privacy, but beware of hemming a small space in, creating too much shade and a damp, dark atmosphere. An open fence or screen will allow air movement – vital in hot, humid climates. Equally, a breezy, cooler outdoor living area can become a protected haven with a little planning. By using reinforced clear glass you can still enjoy the feeling of being out in the garden,

26. Trench garden.	**27.** Chinese garden.

28. Tall screens.

29. Birch screens.

29 Made from the branches of silver birch trees, these screens at the Chaumont-sur-Loire Garden Festival, 2006 are perfectly in keeping with the lightly forested setting.

30 This cube of stiff, clashing, dry bamboo suspended in the middle of a grove of bendy, rustling, living bamboo plants challenges our senses and makes us appreciate the qualities of this versatile screening material.

31 Random piles of flat, creamy sandstone provide a substantial, natural-looking baseline to a lightly screening bambo hedge.

without being buffeted by wind. This is especially useful where a fence is essential for safety reasons but you want to retain the view – near a swimming pool or a steep drop with the ocean beyond.

To make your garden feel larger and part of its setting, cut a porthole out of a hedge or a wall to reveal a desirable view, or to frame a particular aspect of it and direct the eye further afield. You can use the same principle by placing an arch over a plain wooden gate and then cutting a half circle out of the gate below to make a complete circle. A similar effect of framing views can be obtained by building a large line of squares or rectangles, like an oversized trellis on the top of a solid fence, stepping them down to fence level progressively. A clinging climber will soften the effect but needs regular trimming so that you can see through the holes. Once you have the basic material sorted out, there remains the treatment to consider. Concrete block, for example, can be plastered and painted or colour-washed for a

30. Bamboo song.	**31.** Bamboo rock.

32 A large container set in the wall behind this spa pool is filled with ferns and the bright globes of the South African bulb (*Scadoxus multiflorus*), which thrives in the shade.

33 An early design by Ted Smyth relies on the effect of neon lights and stainless steel to turn a plain wall into a work of art.

34 The brilliant colours used for the walls of this display garden at the Ellerslie Flower Show receded in the evening when subtle lighting produced a totally different effect.

Mediterranean look. Make sure you do it properly, though, or the outlines of the blocks will start to show and make it look cheap and nasty. Rough-cast concrete, where you can see the marks of the planks used to make it, can produce an attractive textured effect that complements modern architecture.

Containers for plants can be built in or attached to walls if they are strong enough. Wood can be stained or painted or left to weather naturally. The truly artistic may want to launch into mosaic creations or painted views as a way of decorating their new vertical canvases. In a small garden, mirrors can be a huge asset, placed on a wall to reflect striking plants, pots and sculpture. If you frame them with climbing plants it can be difficult to tell where reality ends and illusion sets in.

In any setting, plants will serve to soften the hard line of a wall or fence and stop a smaller enclosed space from becoming claustrophobic. In fact, by disguising the fence, they will make the garden seem larger. To screen an eyesore, it may be better to place a fine tall tree (or several) strategically, well within your boundary, than to build what will amount to a prison fence. You can also use a strong ground pattern to offset an overwhelming feeling of enclosure, as its strength will draw the eye away from the vertical barrier.

32. Lilac wall.	**33.** Neon wall.

34. Coloured screens.

Hard or soft – the options are vast in both camps. What you cover the ground with has to work in a practical sense, but it can please the eye too.

ground

1. Distant hut.

① (Previous page) A small hut becomes an object of intense interest, placed as it is on the far side of a vast expanse of gently sloping lawn bordered by dense bush.

② A chequerboard pattern of paving and grass draws the eye to the far corner of this garden in Auckland. Designed by Trish Bartleet, it invites visitors to explore as well as giving the lawn a defining border.

③ Sculptor Rick Rudd has created a vivid image of the dramatic effects of a meteor impact, with these papa rock orbs at the entrance to his home in Castlecliff, Wanganui.

④ Leo Jew designed this giant-sized pergola running out from the conservatory at Mana Lodge, Hawke's Bay. The proportions relate to the wider landscape and throw equally magnificent shadows.

The ground is the basis of your garden, the cornerstone of its design, as every other element is built upon it. As the land around our houses becomes more and more restricted and therefore increasingly precious, we need to place greater emphasis on how we treat this rare commodity. The quarter-acre section, mostly in grass, is rapidly becoming a thing of the past and is now more likely to be found in the country. In city gardens it is frequently being replaced by paving.

Soft landscaping includes lawns, groundcovers and all other plant material while paths, steps, terraces and decks constitute the hard or built landscape, along with water receptacles in the form of ornamental or swimming pools. Local by-laws usually restrict the amount of hard surfaces permitted, so that rain-water can soak straight back into the ground instead of going into the storm-water drainage system.

The kind of floor treatment that works inside – a plain, unchanging surface such as a run of the same carpet, polished wood or concrete throughout the house, does not translate readily to the outdoor setting. If we spread exactly the same monotonous surface outside, it would inevitably look dull and

2. Chequerboard lawn.	**3.** Impact garden.

4. Pergola shadows.

5. Oval lawn.

6. Rug lawn.

7. Geomeric patterns.

5 Designed by architect Lucy Treep, this oval lawn has a soothing yet defining shape, providing a large expanse of green to offset the planted borders as well as the sandstone paving.

6 Extending out from the living area, this rug-like lawn turns the courtyard space into an outside living room.

7 Christchurch designer Marion Morris has varied the standard chequerboard lawn pattern to produce a pleasingly random courtyard.

8 Philip Stray of Melbourne decided this yin and yang lawn was meant to be when a circle of Kentucky blue grass he had planted was partially overtaken by kikuyu. When the latter turned yellow in winter the shape revealed itself, so he defined the curves with board and added the mosaic pebble dots.

9 Juan Grimm designed these gently tiered steps at the corner of a sloping lawn at Chiñihue, a garden of vast proportions in Melipilla, Chile.

boring. Look out the window and imagine an endless expanse of leaden grey like a parking lot. Not an inspiring image?

So, make the most of this chance to play with patterns on the ground, especially if you look over the garden from some of the rooms, or from a terrace attached to the house. A knot garden of your combined initials or a pebble mosaic might look amazing from above. What about blending some natural tones with paving and pebbles, or weaving a maze-like pattern with a single line of bricks through concrete aggregate? Embedded flat in concrete, a swirling fern frond or koru shape or a sail of river stones can be truly elegant, and you can use it to focus on or point towards a special feature. Your garden is entirely personal: if you want to insert an astrological sign or two, or to outline your favourite animal, go ahead and do it. Be aware, though, that a strong, full-on pattern will fight with a busy planting arrangement, so take into account the overall effect and make sure you can live with the result in the long term.

8. Yin and yang lawn. | **9.** Grass steps.

10. Mondo lawn.

David Brundell of Gardenza in Glenbrook, south of Auckland, has used trouble-free green and black mondo grass (*Ophiopogon japonicus*) to cover this sloping lawn at his home.

⓫ Aggregate paving stones set in a base of river stones and edged with black mondo grass make an attractive and hard-wearing pathway in the superlative Japanese Garden, Bloedel Reserve, Bainbridge Island, Washington.

⓬ Warm, honey-coloured paving stones interspersed with pebbles of a similar shade are a clever way to blend a trio of silver birches into the setting.

Just as a pair of smart, stylish shoes will set off the rest of an outfit, the material you use on the ground and how it is presented will lay the foundation for everything else you build or grow. It may seem a bit like paying good money for a boring household item no one ever notices, but a sound, solid foundation is essential and will always be money well spent. The ground has an unnerving habit of moving over time, especially with today's erratic climate, and you don't want to be greeted one morning by a sagging path or a huge crack in the paving that the use of better materials or the services of an experienced landscaper might have prevented. If you can't afford it straight off, just do the bare minimum on areas that are in constant use and wait until more affluent times for the rest of the garden. After all, converted grass paddocks, rolled, mowed and cared for, served the previous generations extremely well.

Many people still rate a lawn highly despite the need for maintenance, as nothing else quite matches that smooth green sward for setting off the rest of the garden, quite apart from the unique feeling of grass under bare feet. You can't beat lawns as a place to kick a ball around, play backyard cricket or practise handstands and cartwheels. Stretching out on a rug you've placed under a tree on the lawn is

| **11.** Stepping stones. | **12.** Pavers and pebbles. |

13 The ancient art of mosaic can lift an ordinary pathway to colourful new heights, as shown here in Josie Martin's garden, Akaroa.

14 Instead of being laid flat on their sides, these stones have been placed virtually upright, creating a fascinating texture and look in this Canterbury courtyard.

15 Landscape designer Made Wijaya was responsible for this streamlined ground treatment at the Tirtha Uluwata wedding venue, near the Uluwatu Temple, Bali.

a totally different experience from relaxing on the deck in a lounger. To give your lawn a fresh, modern look, try adding bold patterns and shapes by planting different varieties of grass or groundcover or by breaking up the surface with paving stones. Mow it to create a circular labyrinth, leaving the gaps longer, or just make old-fashioned stripes or diagonals. For inspiration, check out the immaculately groomed and manicured sports fields shown on television.

Lawns will struggle in damp, shady areas and will probably revert to moss or some congenial weed. Neither are they suitable for high traffic areas, where they will turn to mud or dust. Unless you use a desert grass, they will also need a lot of water in the summer months. If a lawn is a must, it will pay you to research grass varieties, as many more rugged, hard-wearing mixes have come on the market in recent years and there are plenty of experts in the field to advise you.

If your particular patch is just too small or unsuitable for lawn, there are plenty of paving solutions – predominately stone, brick or concrete, or softer versions like gravel, pebbles, crushed shell, shingle or bark. Colours vary enormously, depending on the type of rock available, and you can create some

13. Mosaic path.	**14.** Upright stones.

15. Grid pattern.

16. Boardwalk.

16 Anthony Paul's reverence for the atmospheric possibilities of water is amply illustrated by this mossy boardwalk and waterlily-covered pond in his own garden, designed with the sculpture collection of his wife Hannah Peschar in mind.

17 For his award-winning design at the Ellerslie Flower Show, 2004, Alex Schanzer used aluminium checker plates as stepping stones set in a pebble base in the path that wends its way towards a pair of sculptural panels. Lights shine through the laser-cut nikau fronds at night.

18 Christchurch landscaper Ian Fryer designed this garden to become progressively softer, moving beyond a bridge made of slab off-cuts from gravestones, to a sleeper corduroy path flanked by Purpurea (*Acaena inermis*), a useful native groundcover.

17. The Artist's Garden.	**18.** Stone path.

interesting effects by combining large stones and fine gravel in similar tones. Pale colours can become too glary in bright sunlight so they are better used in shady areas where they can lighten up the space.

Whatever the size of your garden, you will need some hard, durable surfaces to use as outdoor seating and dining areas and to provide ways of getting around the property in all weathers. When deciding on a paving pattern or design, you should look to the architecture and materials of your house. A contemporary concrete aggregate, for example, will blend smoothly with a modern house, whereas more traditional stone paving or brick might be preferable outside an older-style home. A fussy mixture will make a small courtyard look even smaller, so keep it simple.

Paths draw the eye and lead us on a journey through the garden. Consider all the possibilities before you set to and start pouring concrete. Do you prefer gentle curving lines or a formal symmetrical layout? If your garden is in the country or by the sea, you might prefer a relaxed, more natural look. You need to be able to move around the garden in comfort without worrying about tripping on an uneven or insecure surface. Most of us glance down as we walk along and if these little glimpses are rewarded by a pleasing appearance, so much the better.

A modern take on the old-fashioned stepping stone, laying plain pavers in a circular, square or diamond shape through a bed of gravel, will suit almost any style of architecture. In a natural country garden, old hardwood logs sawn through to make pennies will look more at home. Make sure they are not too slippery in the wet by leaving them with a bit of texture intact.

19 Isabelle Greene's artistic gifts and sensitive touch result in the creation of enduring landscapes like this superb answer to the need for a dry garden in California.

20 A haphazard arrangement of stepping stones made of granite off-cuts from gravestones works well with native groundcover plants in a coastal location. The addition of a glass and stone sculpture is by the owner John Edgar.

21 Look at what evolves when brave clients allow exceptional designers to follow their intuition! This original garden by Vladimir Sitta in Mosman, Sydney, has become an Australian landscaping icon.

Cost will be an important factor in decisions about ground treatment. Lawn may appear to be a cheap option until you take into account the weekly mowing, weed control and watering that may be needed to keep it looking at its best. Stone paving will be the most expensive but also the most durable and it will become increasingly attractive as it ages. The many and varied concrete options now available may serve your purposes just as well for a smaller outlay, although some can become discoloured and patchy looking in time.

Wooden decking and boardwalks can transform a tiny or unusable space by providing good access out over a garden or down into it so that you feel you are surrounded by plants. Sometimes they are the only feasible way to introduce access or level spaces outside the house. The secret is to balance the built platforms with clever planting to soften and humanise the area, turning it into an enticing outdoor room. What about making one side of the deck moveable so that you can slide parts of it backwards and forwards to catch the sun if it doesn't last long in an area you want to use more. This can be achieved using a railway track arrangement but the trick is to get the balance right and make each panel easy to move while at the same time solid enough to walk and sit on when there are several people using it.

19. Slate and gravel.

20. Natural look.

21. Red garden.

22. Rocks galore.

22 The bold yet subtle use of submerged rocks in the ground surrounding this famous swimming pool is testimony to the innovative vision of California designer Isabelle Greene.

23 A naturalistic stream by designer Peter Nixon in Mona Vale, New South Wales, shows how effective well-thought out planting can be in cementing a new feature into the existing landscape.

24 These diagonal rock lines rise out of the planted border before dropping down to cross the path, at once blending into the landscape and drawing the eye with their inventiveness.

Low, clipped hedges of box or lonicera can accent steps or the edges of ornamental pools by creating strong green lines to offset the cold, hard look of paving. The result can be a sharply defined, structured look that integrates well with most styles of architecture, without being too harsh. The use of mondo grass in between pavers works on the same principle, adding texture and life to break up the rigidity of the stone or concrete.

Steps are a feature in themselves and should be generously wide and shallow to make for ease of movement up and down. By introducing a change of level, they immediately add another dimension – a signal that you are moving through into another part of the garden. They create an opportunity for adding pot plants, either in pairs at the top or bottom, or up each side. You can also use steps to draw

23. Water feature.	**24.** Random lines.

25. Blossom Court.

26. Mosaic path.

27. Crazy paving.

28. Frangipani mosaic.

29. Pebble mosaic.

25 Different coloured pebbles have been laid in a traditional pattern in the Chinese Scholar's Garden, part of the Paradise Garden Collection at Hamilton Gardens.

26 The intriguing pattern of this intricate pebble inlay Tree of Life path in designer Philip Stray's own garden was inspired by a design by St Vigneron's.

27 The gleam of a few randomly placed, brightly coloured tiles leads the eye along this path that runs between stone borders filled with bromeliads and subtropical plants.

28 A traditional frangipani pattern in smooth charcoal and white pebbles lifts this water feature right out of suburbia and into the more exotic world of the tropics.

29 This extensive and beautifully executed design by master craftsman Mark Davidson graces the entrance to Western Park, Ponsonby, Auckland.

30 What an inviting picture this is, with its labyrinth design of sawn bluestone and pebble paving laying the base for a delightful outdoor entertaining room beneath a vine-covered pergola.

attention to a piece of sculpture by placing it at a height. They can be very grand sweeping affairs, suitable for a palace, or very simple and rustic, with railway sleepers and gravel or old bricks.

Water is an exciting medium to add to your groundwork, opening up all kinds of possibilities. Changes in level are perfect for rippling rills where the water flows down narrow channels in a stepped fashion. On a flat site, you can add interest to the base of the rill in the form of pebbles or coloured glass and tiles glistening through the water.

Dark pools will look dramatic at all times of the year, as the sky and vegetation around them transform their smooth surfaces into painted mirages. Lying flat on the ground and taking up a good deal of the surface, a large pool will be dramatic, but you can get the same effect in miniature with a small container – what the French call a miroir d'eau. Dye the water black or line the pot with a black medium to make it reflect more dramatically.

A natural or ornamental pool is endlessly fascinating. You can spend hours keeping an eye out for Jeremy Fisher the frog on the water lily pads or watching the tadpoles grow and change if the kingfisher

30. Pebble courtyard.

31 Lush planting and red lighting zapped this city garden, inspired by pop culture, firmly into the twenty-first century. With its fresh emphasis on colour, texture and shape, it proved an exciting drawcard at the Chelsea Flower Show, 2004.

32 Created by Anne Coney, this inspired mosaic design using tile off-cuts gives her terrace overlooking the sea an endlessly fascinating surface.

33 The sharp contrast in both colour and pattern between these diamond risers and the terracotta tiles equates to very well-accessorised steps.

34 Kevin Kilsby's skill with ceramics and love of colour are evident in these cleverly crafted stepping-stone tiles and the lush foliage of the plants, giving this garden a warmly welcoming atmosphere.

doesn't get them first. The play of light on gently moving water (courtesy of a tiny invisible pump) or the flick of a fish tail will always draw the eye.

A line of river stones or flat pebbles of reasonable size, set into the paving around a pool some distance from the edge like a border or frame, is one of the most enduringly successful treatments.

Pebble mosaics have an ancient fascination that will never fade. They can be appreciated as beautiful works of art or craftsmanship in the same way that, indoors, a designer rug or Persian carpet is a collectible, decorative item.

We all have to start somewhere, however, and anyone can try their hand at making a simple mosaic slab. Work out your pebble pattern first – the simpler the better – and no bigger than 35 cm square. Make a square wooden frame of that size, lay it on a sheet of plastic such as a black rubbish bag and fill with cement, leaving a gap at the top. Push the pebbles into the cement so they lie flat and leave them for a couple of days to dry thoroughly. Then bang the edges as you would to loosen a pot-bound plant and remove the slab. Concrete has to set slowly so that it doesn't shrink or crack, so raise the slab on a bed of sticks to let the air circulate around it, spray it with water once a day for a week and then wait for a month. If you are pleased with the results, do a series of identical ones and use them as stepping stones in gravel.

31. Young at heart.

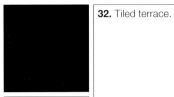

32. Tiled terrace.

33. Diamond steps.

34. Mosaic tiles.

35. Moorish fountain.

35 A traditional star-shaped Moorish fountain, decorated with blue-and-white mosaic tiles, takes centre stage in this courtyard approaching the rose gardens at Lotusland, near Santa Barbara, California.

36 In this playful garden from the Chaumont-sur-Loire Garden Festival, 2006, Botticelli's famous painting *The Birth of Venus* has been cut into puzzle pieces that float on a pond. By chance (or perhaps significantly) this larger piece with Venus's feet standing in a shell has washed up on the shore.

An even simpler approach is to use a plastic food container or tray as a mould. Coat the inside with Vaseline so that it will come out easily like a cake – even more easily if the sides slope outwards slightly. Draw or copy a basic outline – a circle or diamond, number, letter, leaf, ladybird, piglet, whatever – and use that as a template or stencil. Arrange your pieces of glass, stone, buttons, old coins et cetera within the template and then use a cut-out version to outline the shape in the wet concrete, before transferring the pieces to fill it in as pre-arranged. As with making the perfect muffin, much of the secret with concrete lies in the consistency of the mixture. Practice will be required to get it right every time.

Above all, the horizontal or ground plane offers itself up to the artful gardener as a field of fun – a place to experiment and play around with different combinations to see what we like and what will fit in best with the rest of our environment. It's about function, necessarily, but it's also about creativity and the exploration of patterns, textures, colours, shapes, shadows, blends and contrasts, structure and form. Almost anything is possible.

36. Venus's footprint.

We want to commune with nature, but we would prefer to do it in comfort. Today we continue to refine the passion for outdoor living that has molded gardens for centuries.

1. Stage set.

❶ (Previous page) 'Isn't every garden a stage production?' asked the creators of this charming scene at the Chaumont-sur-Loire Garden Festival, 2006. Taking the inside out is a major theme in garden design today.

❷ An ornate old iron seat with a large soft cushion makes a peaceful retreat in Vivienne Papich's garden, Bellevue, at Langs Beach.

❸ Landscape designer Made Wijaya uses subtle colours to create an inviting place to relax in his own garden in Sanur, Bali.

❹ Blue has always been a good choice in the garden as it complements the dominant green of the plants to perfection.

❺ Nothing can beat a splash of yellow to lighten a dark corner and bring sunshine into a garden. Against the dark backdrop, these day lilies add the finishing touch.

Our passion for outdoor living dates back to the earliest gardens. Persian courtyards were sophisticated havens, complete with complex water systems and abundant fruit trees. When the Greeks discovered these pleasure gardens on their conquering forays, they copied them, but it was the Romans who consciously linked their houses and gardens with atriums or courtyards, paths and colonnades, successfully plucking ideas from Greek, Persian and Egyptian gardening traditions.

For inspiration you can still see the Islamic idea of the garden as an earthly paradise in the Moorish gardens of the Alhambra in southern Spain. Gardens might have disappeared altogether during the dark years of the Middle Ages, but for the sheltering walls of the monasteries protecting the utilitarian gardens tended by monks, and the castle fortifications within which pleasure gardens were nurtured. The Renaissance in Italy saw the rebirth of a more formal design or architectural approach to the garden as an extension of the house. This took hold in Europe, fuelled by the grand excesses of monarchs like Louis XIV, until the English ushered in a more relaxed style of picturesque landscape gardening. By the time the Victorian era came along, gardens were once again being incorporated in the house itself,

2. Cosy nook.   **3.** Balinese seat.   **4.** Blue and white.

5. Yellow light.

6. Tree seat.	**7.** Poppy paradise.	**8.** Board seats.
	9. Wooden toadstools.	**10.** Blue iron seats.
11. Seating area.	**12.** Armed bench.	**13.** Colourful cane.

6 Trees draw you to them but unless the owners have thought to add a user-friendly seat like this one in Connecticut, you probably won't linger long enough to enjoy sitting under them.

7 Can you imagine a more romantic setting in which to dine outside? Self-sown poppies abound in this garden in Wanaka, Otago.

8 A garden always looks lived in when chairs and a table are nestled into a corner.

9 These rounded, wooden carved seats by sculptor Alison Crowther look for all the world like overgrown toadstools.

10 An ornate blue iron seat graces the garden at Quinta Nicolasa, Santiago, Chile.

11 This welcoming outdoor area utilises the space on top of a garage situated in the middle of a group of town houses, and offers fresh air and respite to residents.

12 A wooden bench lends itself to the creative spirit and becomes an exercise in physics.

13 An adventurous approach to paint can give an old cane sofa like this one a new lease of life.

14 Focused on a serpentine stainless steel bench set on a central dais and surrounded by a moat of crushed purple Perspex, this smartly executed design carried off the award for best chic garden at Chelsea in 2004.

in the form of ever more elaborate conservatories. These were built to house the exotic plants brought back from the far corners of the globe by intrepid plant hunters.

It was in the 'New World', on the west coast of America, that landscape architect Thomas Church and his followers developed the idea that 'gardens are for people' and launched a form of modernism known as the California style. Established following the depression of the early 1930s, it emphasised the garden as a usable space extending from the house, and became the basis of indoor–outdoor living as we know it today.

Now, in the twenty-first century, we have come full circle and want to live outdoors in much the same way as we live inside our houses. This means making spaces for cooking, eating, playing, resting and

14. Chic garden.

15. Bamboo deck chairs.

16. Pink chairs.

17. Deck chairs.

15 The amazing versatility of bamboo is demonstrated once again by these comfortable deck chairs.

16 These flowing metal chairs with their elegant drink-holders remove the need for a table.

17 Old-fashioned canvas deck chairs will always have a place in the garden as they are colourful, versatile and easy on the eye.

18 Relaxing outside by this pool in Chiñihue Garden, not far from Santa Cruz, offers a taste of luxurious leisure.

relaxing in comfort – with reasonable protection from the elements. Although our outdoor space will work in harmony with the indoors and may repeat some of the patterns and the overall defining style, we look for it to provide an extra element in our lives: a way of connecting with nature.

Everyone needs this balance in their lives – we are not genetically programmed to live in a totally urban environment. We need fresh air and some sort of interaction with plants, animals, birds and insects to refresh ourselves and deal with the stress of everyday life in the modern world. Gardens are therapeutic and shouldn't be seen as a chore or an impossible learning curve; they should be for everyone. If you have an outdoor space, however tiny or unpromising, you can convert it into a place for rejuvenating the spirits and relaxing mind and body after a hard day's work.

The trick lies in how well you can analyse yourself and what you want in that outdoor space. Do you want to dig and delve, mow the lawn, and have the satisfaction of growing ornamental plants for their foliage and flowers – or herbs and vegetables for cooking? Are you in need of a hammock slung in the shade, with a glass of wine at hand? Do you love to entertain and party or is the quiet, contemplative life

18. Poolside living.

19 Dense tropical planting, including water lilies and pitcher plants, softens the semi-industrial setting of this floating garden.

20 This simple bench seat is made especially appealing by the addition of a thick white squab and rolls.

21 Bay trees, clipped into topiary tiers, rising out of sleek black wooden tubs, set the scene for a dreamy outdoor space, complete with cosy Dedon all-weather chair, overlooking Judges Bay in Auckland Harbour.

for you? Do you have young children, or friends who call by regularly with theirs in tow? Perhaps you have a pet or two needing to be accommodated.

Once you have that lot sorted, decide what type of garden will supply most of the things on your wish list. It could well be that a fresh coat of paint, a recycled chair and a few undemanding pot plants will be enough to satisfy your longings for paradise. But it is also possible that once you get bitten by the gardening bug, you will want to create something that really works to supply everything on that wish list. Often the easiest and most practicable way of going about it is to replicate the basic style you have chosen to use inside, but in a bolder, braver fashion. Out of doors you will no doubt feel more liberated and so the decorating process will be easier and much more low-key, with the emphasis on enjoyment and pleasure – for you.

In an ideal world, house and garden would be designed concurrently, so that each interacted seamlessly with the other. Instead of the house being a large block in the middle of the garden, the two would share the space, with courtyards and gardens appearing within and around the overall architectural plan for indoor spaces, rather like the Roman ideal. If this opportunity has passed, you can

| **19.** Tropical living. | **20.** Poolside rest. |

21. Love seat.

22 Who wouldn't feel comfortable in this circular seating area with its welcoming soft cushions and solar-powered rill? This ecologically sustainable contemporary garden was designed by Hadrian Whittle for the Hampton Court Palace Flower Show, 2006.

23 Persian rugs and cushions make this small space ideal for a gathering of a few friends for a quiet gossip.

24 Melbourne designer Jim Fogarty has used bluestone cobbles to soften this pool area, made more inviting by recliners and a soothing water feature and wall hanging.

25 A bit of artistic flair goes a long way in designer Rae Jones-Evans's own garden in Melbourne. This simple frame, festooned with sheer pink curtains, shows how easy it can be when you know how.

often make amends by inserting large doors and windows that clearly invite people outside. Glass can have the effect of doubling the size of your deck or outdoor space by reflecting it. If the weather is bad, you can still feel as though you are outside in a green, airy world. Waking up in a bedroom where the garden lies before you in the morning sun, or watching the lights and stars at night, are among life's greatest pleasures. If you can step outside to sit down and enjoy that morning cup of coffee or evening glass of wine away from prying eyes, so much the better.

Beautiful views are not available to everyone, but you can always create your own within the boundaries of your garden. Think of it as a stage set upon which you will compose an ideal scene, complete with paths, steps, maybe an arch or pergola, dripping with climbers, ornaments, plants, water and possibly even a painted vista or seascape on that boring concrete wall at the back. Perhaps you have come back from an overseas holiday with a passion for tropical isles and palm trees, or those amazing blues you see in Morocco, from the jacarandas to the house paint. Or have the lavender fields of France or the sunflowers of Eastern Europe got you in their grasp? They may not translate so well to your own

23. Intimate space.	**24.** Pool courtyard.	**25.** Curtained pavilion.

26 Hammocks have long had a well-earned reputation for being the ultimate means of enjoying an afternoon siesta or relaxing with a book in the peaceful shade of a tree or two.

27 Landscaper Brent Reid designed this lush garden, surrounding a Noek Design Deckhouse constructed by Semken Landscaping, for the Melbourne International Flower and Garden Show, 2006.

backyard but at least you have the initial inspiration firmly in your head, and that is a start. One of the great advantages of a garden is that it gives you a wonderful view to look out on from inside. Or at least it should, so keep that in mind when you are deciding what to put there. Sit or stand where you usually spend most of your time then look out, trying to visualise the various possibilities. Include the borrowed landscape of neighbouring gardens but be aware that beautiful trees, for example, may disappear without warning. You only have control over your patch.

Be positive about what you have – a small courtyard can be made cosy and sheltered, whereas a larger space might be divided into several outdoor rooms, more than one used for living on a daily basis, perhaps by different age groups within the family.

If you have the luxury of designing from scratch, bear in mind that outdoor living spaces should

26. Hammock.

27. Forest retreat.

28. Framed view.

28 If your outdoor living space has a fabulous harbour view, why not bring it into focus with a frame, as architects Pip Cheshire and Malcolm Taylor have done with this property.

29 This rear courtyard, designed by Georgina Martyn, incorporates feng shui principles. Almost every element is curved, making it a restful place to be.

30 A garden with a watering system designed to recycle stormwater provides an eco-friendly, guilt-free retreat from the world.

theoretically be larger than those inside to avoid a feeling of pokiness and claustrophobia, but they should still generate a feeling of intimacy and privacy, of being surrounded by a pleasing garden backdrop.

In its simplest form, a generous verandah, deck or terrace can offer outdoor living space. Ideally, it should have some form of overhead shelter from the heat of the sun and from falling rain – an awning or sail can be perfectly adequate. With larger houses, a loggia might be an option, consisting of a complete room open to the air on one, two or more sides, usually with cooking facilities and sofas and chairs. For ease of movement, it makes sense to locate an outdoor area that will be used primarily for entertaining and dining close to the main living area and kitchen of the house. You will also want to catch the last rays of the setting sun to make the most of summer's long evenings, and that may mean you have to place your outdoor living area further away. You will need to examine your priorities and make an appropriate decision.

| **29.** Feng shui. | **30.** Raingarden. |

31. Urban simplicity.

31 This peaceful outdoor dining area has all the elements required for a restorative space – water and a single well-chosen tree underplanted with enough soothing green to offset the hard surfaces.

32 The four fundamentals of a Japanese garden – water, stone, plants and human senses – are incorporated alongside contemporary materials in this Zen garden.

33 The use of strong architectural plant-forms creates a year-round backbone for this cool and restful garden, which uses economical and functional materials in an inventive way.

Fragrant plants are often much more potent in the evening so make the most of them. In a warm climate you could grow gardenias, star jasmine, the unprepossessing but heavenly night-scented Jessamine (*Cestrum nocturnum*), or even frangipani if it is hot enough. In more temperate zones try sweet peas, roses, lavender, scented-leaf pelargoniums and lilies. Frost-tender citrus trees have been grown in containers for centuries in Europe, but can cope in the ground in a reasonably sheltered spot. They have everything you could want in a plant – thick green foliage, scented blossom and deliciously refreshing sun-like fruit in vibrant oranges and yellows. Alternatively you could try cool, crisp, green limes.

To replace a labour-intensive lawn, use a mixture of paving and gravel to make a smaller area more interesting, and intersperse it with mondo grass for some cool, green, grass-like texture. In surrounding shady areas, use baby's tears or mind-your-own-business, Soleirolia soleirolii, but not where it will get walked on. Likewise Scleranthus biflorus (Canberra grass), which makes wonderful mossy mounds in full sun.

32. Niwazare.	**33.** Immaculate square.

34 What better place to entertain friends than in the comfort and welcoming shade provided by this cool terrace at Chiñihue Garden, Melipilla, Chile.

35 This deep, generous verandah offers relief from the sun, while making visitors feel as if they are up in the canopy of the palms and other trees looking out over widespread views of the garden and beyond.

36 Stylish outdoor dining in among the potted plants makes for a novel feature near the restaurant at the Chaumont-sur-Loire Garden Festival, 2006.

34. Chiñihue Garden.	**35.** Treetop view.

If your outdoor space consists of a roof or balcony you will need to use tough plants that can cope with wind and atmospheric pollution. Soil is heavy so you might be severely restricted in the amount you can use in containers, which should be light but firmly secured in place. Balconies are usually smaller but more exposed, so you might want to add a screen or two where appropriate.

While outdoor kitchens and barbecues have always made sense in warm climates and somehow food always tastes better out of doors, outdoor fireplaces have also become popular where the temperature drops sharply once the sun disappears. They can be sharply contemporary with long, clean lines, or highly individual with tiles or other decoration, depending on the owner's whim. A long hearth extending either side can be extremely useful for extra seating, but remember to add cushions as concrete can be unforgiving. If entertaining is your prime purpose, the fireplace can include a rotisserie iron for roasting. Just like an old-fashioned open fire inside the house, the flames create a unique atmosphere and magnetic focal point, perfect for a group gathering.

A more affordable option is a simple brazier, which will cast a cheerful light and give out plenty of warmth. Tall gas heaters like those used outdoors at restaurants will extend the time you are able to spend outside as well.

37. Sunny haven.

37 Even in early spring this sunny spot beckons you outside to enjoy dining al fresco in the warmth of the sun.

38 Cheerful cushions from Central Asia and a bright striped tablecloth make this Melbourne courtyard a delightful place in which to spend time.

39 A fresh white backdrop, enlivened by blue and yellow furnishings, is kept cool by a grapevine-covered pergola.

40 A view of the ocean often comes with a less welcome sea breeze, but shelter is on hand here with these adjustable shutters.

38. Cushioned retreat.	**39.** White-washed alcove.
40. Shuttered sanctuary.	

41 With these clear glass panels, you can relish the feeling of sitting outside in this sunny courtyard within the garden, while still being totally protected from any unpleasant breezes.

42 Dining outside on this stunning terrace would establish a cheerful, convivial atmosphere even without the addition of company.

43 Located beside a wine cellar, this entertainers courtyard continues the theme: from the vine overhead, to the traditional European fan pattern for the cobblestones underfoot, and the table and pot decorated with grapes.

The choice of outdoor furniture has positively exploded in the last decade. While traditional wood and iron will always look right in a classic garden, they have their drawbacks and are not always comfortable unless padded out with cushions. Iron can also get unpleasantly hot if it is in full sun so be careful where you put it. French café-style chairs are making a huge comeback – the more worn and authentic looking the better, although they are more for show than long leisurely dining experiences.

Wood is a remarkably amenable material and can take on a myriad looks and uses including the humble, enduring deck-chair; the director's chair (moveable backs make all the difference here); the Adirondack or Cape Cod chair – now available with a matching footstool in the smartest stores; solid hardwood chairs to match outdoor tables; slatted reclining deck-chairs like those used on ocean liners a century ago; benches – curved and straight, old church pews, homemade versions using fallen or recycled timber – the list is endless. We all have our favourites and they are in no danger of disappearing in the near future.

41. Clear protection.

42. Art work.

43. Grape arbour.

44. Tiled fireplace.

44 Nothing draws people together more easily than an open fire like this outdoor one, designed to warm diners enjoying a meal in this Canterbury garden.

45 A variation on the usual barbecue becomes an attractive focal point to this outdoor garden in the inner city.

46 Lush tropical plants make this outdoor entertaining area feel warm, even without the modern fireplace with its welcoming hearth that doubles as extra seating.

However, plastic and synthetic fibres now provide a much more broad-based and practical alternative to those delightful cane and wicker chairs that once sat in your grandmother's conservatory and that puppies love to chew on. At the top end of the scale, these new versions are the last word in elegance and durability. You can buy exact replicas of the old colonial cane and wicker furniture so evocative of Somerset Maugham and steamy tropical nights spent sipping pink gin slings, or you can inject an aura of ultimate modern chic in the form of up-to-the-minute loungers and armchairs. Modular arrangements allow you to put separate pieces together to create whatever combination you want. Light and easy to move, they also dry out quickly, making them ideal near swimming pools or anywhere exposed to regular downpours. Even long exposure to the sun and salty sea air shouldn't do much more than produce a slight change of colour.

For a permanent outdoor setting, polished concrete is an excellent alternative to a stone table. If you want something that is lighter than traditional stone, you can now buy a mixture of fibreglass and stone that looks exactly like the real thing. Such furniture is relatively easy to move, which is a huge plus.

45. Copper barbecue.

46. Tropical dining.

47 The surviving chimney from a house fire was pressed into service in a remodelled version to add extra warmth to this outdoor dining area.

48 A Kerikeri couple had this highly practical antique barbecue made as a back-up for entertaining large groups of friends.

49 The possibilities for dining outside at this restored villa are greatly enhanced, courtesy of the heat bestowed by a carefully moulded fireplace.

It might also be feasible to consider using low walls and steps of concrete, stone or brick as extra seating. Wooden benches can be used in the same way, purpose-built around wooden decks.

One of the most exciting aspects of designing a space for living outdoors is that you can be much more flexible with shape than is practical indoors. You can, for example, explore the use of curved shapes such as ovals or semi-circles in your seating and wall or screen plans, to create a pleasant feeling of enclosure and protection.

More than anything else, the most important factor in designing your garden with outdoor living in mind is to make it inviting. Somehow you must create a mood or an atmosphere that draws people out into the air. This can be as simple as a shady pergola creating welcome respite from the heat of a summer's day, or conversely, a bright, sunny spot that makes you want to sit outside when the weather is cooler. To be inviting it must look comfortable and attractive, just like a living room indoors. Think about what works for you in that sphere and have fun creating an outdoor oasis that has the bonus of being surrounded by living, changing plants to add colour, texture and interest.

47. Recycled chimney.

48. Designer barbecue.

49. Glowing
heat.

By capturing our attention and providing focus to a landscape, sculpture adds to our appreciation of it. Placement is therefore of paramount importance to our enjoyment of both art and nature.

sculpture

1. Orb,

2. Farm scene.

❶ (Previous page) Gary Baynes' background as a sheet metal engineer has given him the practical skills to express his artistic vision and produce works like this galvanised, powder-coated and lacquered orb.

❷ Rising out of the sculpture forest at Rannoch, this mixed media sculpture by Paul Millin is part of the James Wallace Arts Trust collection.

❸ A lonely figure cast in bronze by Palmerston North sculptor Paul Dibble looks out to sea from the Ravenscar Garden at Taylor's Mistake, Christchurch.

❹ The powerful Pacific figures Haeata and Porehu by Paul Dibble represent Dawn and Dusk after Michelangelo's *Tomb for the Medici.*

The passion for filling gardens with sculpture is not new. Renaissance gardens in Italy are full of stone figures inspired by ancient Greece and Rome. Classic gardens throughout Europe continued the trend, in a formal setting near the house, and in temples and grottoes further afield.

Such classical pieces are still popular and have their place, particularly in traditional formal gardens. In the last few decades, however, sculpture of an entirely different kind has proliferated, with sculpture parks and gardens appearing around the world at an amazing rate. This is not a renaissance because the artists do not look back to past civilisations for inspiration – they take whatever strikes them as being worthy or of interest from contemporary life. Nor are they necessarily formed from traditional stone,

| **3.** The Long Wait. | **4.** Haeata and Porehu. |

5 A reclining woman by Bronwynne Cornish merges with the ground beneath her and will inevitably be slowly covered by the surrounding plants.

6 David McCracken's stainless steel sculpture *Flukes and Margins #6* in Tom Mutch's Coromandel garden draws power from the unlikely tension between the solid strength of the metal and the softer, curved forms it has been forced into.

7 Arms with upturned palms by sculptor Helen Pollock rise out of Lake Pupuke, giving rise to all kinds of emotional responses in the viewer.

8 This sculpture by Terry Stringer stands at the edge of a lake in Frank and Vicki Boffa's garden in Waikanae.

marble, bronze, wood or clay, although they may be. These days they can be made of glass, wire, welded metal, ceramics, plastic or some other synthetic material. Colour, movement and even sound may be integral, often transforming a piece into something far from its basic form.

Why this huge resurgence of interest in sculpture out of doors? Perhaps it is no more than a desire to have every aspect of our indoor lives replicated or enhanced and expanded outside. Like a wall without a painting, a pleasantly planted garden may lack that extra something to give it that indefinable edge and draw the eye . But while we may love a piece of sculpture or fine ornament, it must be right for its place. If it doesn't suit the setting, much of its inherent strength will be lost, and the viewer will be left with a feeling that nature might well have been better left unadorned.

Out in the open, the integration of art with nature seems to bring that art to life more vividly than is possible inside a building. Besides, the outdoors can accommodate a vast increase in scale. In a park or garden we can enjoy sculptural pieces of a dimension that would be impossible to experience properly

5. The Dreamer.

6. Flukes and Margins #6.

7. Wave.

8. Behind the studio screen.

9. Deity heads.

9 Lying on the gravel beneath a tree in the Hannah Peschar Sculpture Garden, these disembodied deity heads by Patricia Volk fascinate even as they horrify – who, what, why?

10 In this sculpture, Patricia Volk has captured something of the inner mystery of a woman's head, its sheer simplicity suggesting inner knowledge of a spiritual truth.

11 These sculptures by Terry Stringer could have no finer setting than the natural theatre provided by Zealandia at Mahurangi West, north of Auckland.

in an enclosed space. The constantly changing patterns of natural light, further enhanced at night by artificial light, can also add a sense of vibrancy to what might otherwise be a dull, unresponsive surface.

Some sculpture parks or gardens are permanent collections, privately owned or attached to a museum or botanical garden. Others exhibit works for sale: sometimes these properties are owned by the sculptor and work in effect as a display garden. Still others invite known artists to create a work for a specific place on their land, or even give them the freedom to choose the site.

None of this comes cheaply of course but even if you can't imagine being able to afford a single piece for your garden at this point in time, it is worth planning your garden with a view to that becoming a reality. Because placement is of paramount importance in getting the maximum amount of enjoyment from any piece, you may find it useful to employ a landscape designer, who will often suggest appropriate places and incorporate them in your garden plans. They can also point you in the direction of various sculptors and may even accompany you to exhibitions to assist with the final selection.

10. Yellow head.   **11.** Zealandia.

12. Glass sculpture.

13. Pou whenua.

14. Pierced heart.

12 Meryn Saccente's glass spears are a distinctive focal point in a water feature at the entrance to a garden in Glendowie, Auckland.

13 Powerful simplistic figures by Arnold Wilson illustrate his belief that traditional Maori carving should be reinterpreted and reinvigorated to give it new energy and life.

14 Far from the colourful, cupid-like image it appears to be, Para Matchitt's symbolic heart, pierced by an arrow, harks back to the New Zealand Wars of the 1860s.

15 A chillier interpretation of Matchitt's hearts in stainless steel is again based on a redemption symbol flown on flag pennants by Maori fighting to retain their rights.

Just as hard landscaping in the form of paving, walls and built elements stays exactly the same, providing structure throughout the changing seasons, so too will your sculpture remain a constant feature over time. The plants around it will grow and change but your pivotal piece will not. That is another reason for sensitive placement as although it may appear more prominent or less, depending on the changing nature of the plants around it, a dominant piece is not easily moved and you want it to be as effective as possible.

Garden centres offer a range of smaller and more affordable works to choose from. It is also worth visiting as many exhibitions and specialist galleries as you can to find the work of a sculptor that appeals to you. Be aware that what looks amazing in a large park or similar setting may not work in the same way at all in a domestic context. But small gardens can cope with a single substantial piece and that is often a wiser approach than filling tight spaces with masses of tiny, unrelated bits that may lead to a claustrophobic feeling of clutter. Place a lone sculpture of your choice at the end of a path in the distance, raise it on a plinth or a solid block, frame it in some way with plants or a structure, and stand back to

15. Heart within a heart.

16. Water lilies.

16 Twirling gently on the lake at Brick Bay Sculpture Trail, these delicate corrugated iron 'lilies' by Jeff Thomson take on the air of ballet dancers or ice skaters.

17 A whimsical frog fountain brings a splash of water to a dry, succulent garden designed by Jenny Smith Gardens of Melbourne.

18 A Jeff Thomson sculpture at Smiths' House, Waiheke, is created out of twisted and rusting pieces of old corrugated iron, a sharp contrast to the modern house behind, which is newly built of the same material.

enjoy the effect. As objects look smaller in the distance, you are using that sense of illusion to make the garden look larger than it actually is. A smaller simple pot or something like a chair, brightly coloured pole or tripod – placed off to the side, partway down the path – will create a balanced feeling and another point of interest. By introducing another angle, it will also make the space seem larger.

One classical item passed down from antiquity that always manages to look right is a simple terracotta urn or large pot. If you feel bereft of ideas and have trouble deciding on an ornament or sculpture to suit your garden, you can't go far wrong with one of these or a beautiful contemporary version.

Best of all, a striking piece well placed will mean that all kinds of mishaps and lack of husbandry in the adjacent beds will go unnoticed. Strong focal points get people moving and they will trot past your weeds and overlook the deadheads just to get to the end of the path and look at that urn. Use such objects to manage your garden and bring an element of control and surprise. Having got to the end of the path, visitors will appreciate a seat or just a simple bench on which to sit and look back, otherwise it will be a

| **17.** Frog fountain. | **18.** Smith's House. |

19 Nestled by the pool in a Herne Bay garden, this large, laser-cut stainless steel sculpture is indicative of Virginia King's concern for the environment, especially in relation to the sea and the life within it.

20 The delicate and beautiful form of a feather is captured in glass, stainless steel and polycarbonate by Neil Dawson, in the Becroft Garden, Lake Pupuke.

21 Sculptor Virginia King draws attention to the beauty and fragility of the flax snail, an endangered species, treasured creature and living fossil. By making it look enormous and yet frail we are forced into awareness of its deadly plight.

22 One of two sculptures made by Virginia King in support of the Women's Refuge for Sculpture OnShore, 2004. Inspired by both vessels and palm leaf fronds the stainless steel sculpture appears to have been welded together by latticework along the spine.

fast trip there and back. This is where focal points are useful to break up the journey through a garden – they give your visitors a chance to pause and truly appreciate what they see instead of charging on to finish the race to nowhere.

An entirely different atmosphere will result if you place your prized possession, a tallish terracotta or richly glazed urn, within the planting at the edge of a curving path. The urn will still draw the eye and set the viewer in motion along the path towards it, but by making the line curve and settling the focal piece in a more relaxed manner within the garden itself, you will have created a totally different, more contemplative mood. Discreet placement will add to the delights of discovery a garden offers and it is worth trying to see if you can include this element of surprise.

Wall plaques are another way of adding interest to a small garden as they fit neatly on the vertical

19. Nautilus Whispers.

20. Little Vanity.

21. Pupu Harakeke.

22. Waitemata Frond.

23 Set against the tall trunks of young kauri trees, a bronze detail of karaka leaves and flower buds by Terry Stringer reveals the beauty to be found within New Zealand's native flora.

24 A powerful row of totem-like figures carved out of macrocarpa by sculptor Fatu Feu'u, at the Brick Bay Sculpture Trail.

25 The delicate tracery of decaying mahoe leaves is captured for eternity in these corrugated iron sculptures by Jeff Thomson, lying as if scattered by the wind at Te Whau Garden, Waiheke.

24. Kone Fitu.	**25.** Mahoe Leaves.

plane of a wall, without taking up extra space. You can find copies of antique classics, words and quotes, or colourful mosaic, shell and ceramic plaques to buy ready-made. The block paintings that some artists specialise in would do wonders for an outside wall, if they could be made weatherproof. Many are designed to hang in groups and have much greater presence that way. Photographs can be vastly enlarged and treated for outdoor display as giant hangings or sculptures in their own right. It all comes down to personal choice and the ability to visualise the ultimate effect.

Sundials are making a comeback and some innovative sculptors are creating clever new variations on the theme. You can get vertical and wall dials; bold, colourful sun designs; minimalist wall plaques and even fountain dials where the water jet replaces the gnomon (finger) as the marker of time. Once you get hooked, there are a million ways you can play with the sun and the shadows it casts, using rough-hewn stone as a primitive take on the subject or modern reflective materials like glass or polished metal. The traditional flat circular form based on a pedestal has long been a favourite garden ornament, with its reassuring image of scientific order triumphing over chaos. Armillary sundials, with their three rings and rod or arrow through the centre, are beautifully composed and would look aesthetically pleasing anywhere. They evolved from the celestial globes used by ancient astronomers to plot the position of the stars. (The first ring represents the equator and has the hours marked on it, a second stands for the meridian and a third the horizon.) The rod representing the earth's axis shows the time by casting its shadow on to the hour lines on the equatorial ring. Time is eternally fascinating and you may find it

26 Created for the 100% Pure New Zealand Garden at Chelsea in 2006, the limpet is a symbol of the longing that Kiwis abroad feel for home, referring to the way limpets habitually return to the same rock pool. Perhaps there is also a reference to the pull of the ocean on the Kiwi spirit.

27 In glass and mild steel, these waving 'flowers' by Inge Panneels beckon the viewer to follow the trail they form along this stretch of water at the Hannah Peschar Sculpture Garden.

28 Pauline Rhodes' sculpture at Brick Bay Sculpture Trail is not made or crafted but consists of two coils of flexlock hose – a synthetic material placed in a natural environment – raising all kinds of questions besides challenging our preconceived ideas about sculpture.

26. Piha Limpet.	**27.** Field of Infinity.

rewarding to commission an artist who has specialised in this field to come up with an original piece for your garden on this ancient theme.

Part of the appeal of sculpture is that it can be all things to all people. Some pieces are fun, some clever; others make a point or push a particular agenda. Still others are simply arrestingly beautiful. Kinetic or moving sculptures can be riveting with their cleverly engineered extremities that are specially weighted and balanced to move in the slightest breeze. It is impossible not to be entranced as they move in ever changing patterns, seeming certain to collide but instead gliding past each other with the grace of a ballet.

The human figure has been a traditional subject for sculptural interpretation since the earliest art forms were made. At the beginning of the twenty-first century one discernible trend has developed whereby the body is divided into parts and these are placed so that they interact with the landscape. Some works are literally embedded in the ground, evoking images of mother earth and the fundamental need for human contact with the natural world to which we belong. These images can be lighthearted, even whimsical, or they can be indicative of human frailty when compared with the force of nature. Sometimes they can be downright disturbing as they call to mind images of death and decay.

In some cases the artist may be reminding us of our peril if we continue to destroy the fragile ecological balance of the world around us. On a more personal level, people are universally concerned with their own image, the figure they present to the world, and also with the issue of self-discovery.

28. Two Tangles
Touching.

29. Strange Flowers.

30. Aluminium Grass.

31. Eighteen Piece Toe Toe.

29 Strange yet compelling, these 'flowers' by Phillip Luxton, made out of towering ceramic columns, rise out of the cliff at Tiromoana, Gisborne.

30 Waving on slender stems, Sarah Brill's sculpture looks at home amid the subtropical planting at Landsendt, Oratia, Auckland.

31 Finely textured glass by Phil Newbury catches the sunlight in this recreation of the feathery native toe toe.

32 A sculpture by Andrew Drummond stands like a sentinel below the wall at Ohinetahi, Governor's Bay, Canterbury, while two of Ian Lamont's rusty cabbage trees beckon in the distance.

33 Robert Jahnke has experimented with the strength of his material – wood from the mighty totara tree – by stretching and twisting it, revealing its innate power.

Sometimes such works seek to explore ideas of disintegration and re-assembly, whether of the individual or society, where the whole form is suggested but never presented. Like the missing pieces of a puzzle, the absent parts become a powerful magnet, arousing our curiosity.

Artists working with metal frequently use this medium to represent some of the finer shapes and delicate patterns in our natural environment, drawing our attention to the intricate forms of plants, birds, animals and fish we may have taken for granted. Others use a range of materials, from glass to concrete, to make solid, sometimes bizarre representations of living creatures and plants of giant proportions that demand our attention by their sheer bulk and unnatural proportions. By putting art and nature side by side in this way, the one providing a tactile, visual representation of the other, we are forced to look afresh at the natural world around us. The similarities are brought into focus, yet we are reminded that they are quite distinct.

The land itself, together with what it means to us physically and spiritually, has been used throughout the ages by sculptors wanting to draw our attention to the multiple issues involved. Ethnic and cultural

32. Wind sculpture.

33. Rautotara.

34 Matt McLean's sculpture of delicately balanced ceramic blocks with stepped edges has become a focal point in Gil Hanly's Mt Eden garden.

35 Curved sculptures by Barry Brickell, decorated by artist Nigel Brown, border a pathway at Driving Creek Potteries and Railway, just north of Coromandel.

36 Giant balls slide along parallel rods, designed to resemble a game board, on which you can compose your own garden simply by moving the balls.

factors intensify the debate, and act as a powerful stimulus. Set in a cultivated garden, the strength of such works is immediately intensified and we cannot help but respond. On larger properties, huge earth sculptures can create incredible effects, carving out shapes and patterns to represent themes of man's interaction with the land; scientific discovery; or a re-creation and interpretation of other lands' ancient sculptures, which continue to fascinate thousands of years on.

Domesticity and the way people live – from houses to furniture and household items – comprise another popular theme in sculpture. Occasionally, sculptors will be asked to design actual buildings, rather than represent them in some way. Again, unusual materials might be used to create familiar objects, so that they strike us anew.

34. Plunging Fire.	**35.** Collaboration.

36. Flower'n'Roll.

37. Sculpture in the Gardens.

37 Brightly coloured, galvanised steel sculptures by Richard Cooper give a Polynesian-influenced strength and focus to the perennial plants featured in the Botanic Gardens entry at the Ellerslie Flower Show, 2007.

38 Exhibited at Sculpture on the Gulf, 2003, Neil Dawson's painted stainless steel ball has an ethereal quality, with its intricate surface pattern of finely cut out shapes.

39 The perfection of this seemingly solid stainless steel ball by David McCracken is a source of fascination in itself, even before the slits in its surface cast their spell.

The expanding use of found objects since early last century has thrown the field of three-dimensional expression open in an entirely new way. Artists can and do combine objects of all kinds in an imaginative variety of ways. Some of these may strike a chord, appealing to you because of the inherent wit or meaning of the assemblage.

Abstract forms transcend questions of place and time, seeking a more universal or holistic ideal. Often they are based on pure geometric shapes instead of recognisable figures and architectural or natural entities. Balanced by contemporary architecture and landscaping, they can be especially compelling.

Sound is an element in some contemporary sculpture, and that is another aspect to consider outside. If it is interactive you can control it, but if it vibrates, throbs, hums or involves loud music and operates on a set cycle you may find that, like a water feature, it can be far too invasive and constant. At the right

38. Jive Ball.	**39.** Nice Round Figure.

40. Fish skeleton.

40 Kristin Taylor created this ceramic prehistoric fish skeleton in a glass exhibition box in response to archaeological finds unearthed on the site of this Sydney garden.

41 The potentially tragic consequences of our actions as we stand at the crossroads of our ecological future are brought home vividly by sculptor Bing Dawe with *Never Much-Loved Black Shag at the Ox-Bow*, from the Stoneleigh Sculpture in the Gardens exhibition.

42 Made by Rustic Twist, these iconic corrugated iron animals are popular decorative items in the garden.

43 A flock of birds in stainless steel by Fred Graham is startled into flight above a lake. They refer to the Maori belief that birds were the original inhabitants of this land and of their ability to warn of danger, as well as their inherent beauty.

41. Black Shag.

42. Rustic goat.

43. Ohorere – 'to startle'.

44 Fiona Garlick brings into focus the waste threatening the future of our planet by linking these discarded (but once useful) objects, in a giant iron chain reminiscent of a charm bracelet.

45 Peter Lange's perverse sense of humour is evident in his determination to meld brick into a more malleable material, capable of being used to build curving, soft objects and even ones that float.

46 Les Kossatz's life-like sheep sculptures at Coliban near Kyneton, Victoria, make a wry comment on the human condition, via an archetypal image of rural Australia.

pitch and level, it will add to your experience of the space – just make sure you can turn it off for some respite when peace and quiet are needed.

Water, with the added factors of reflection, flotation and sometimes movement, can make an interesting setting for sculpture. Pieces that would merely appear clunky or boring on land take on a new vibrancy when they appear to float or rise out of a more mobile medium, gently ruffled by the wind or smooth and mirror-like. You may not have a large lake at your disposal, but even a tiny water feature will mirror the sky and offer peace and tranquillity. An ornamental or natural pool will have the same effect, albeit on a smaller scale than a lake or pond.

Lighting can have an absolutely magical effect on any sculptural features in the garden and it is well worth the investment. Ideally, the wires should go in when the garden is being constructed but you can have some extra points left to be brought into use for later acquisitions or personal creations. Gardens never remain the same and sculpture is one of the most moveable features so don't feel you have to get it right first time round – unless the piece is large and piped in as part of a water feature or other immoveable structure. A gentle up-light rather than a spotlight is sufficient in most cases, and you will be well rewarded every night when your favourite pieces glow in a new way, taking on a different appearance altogether as the rest of the stage – the garden – is draped in shadow and darkness.

Whatever your circumstances, the potential for sculpture in the form of 'found' or personally created objects is as limitless as your imagination and maybe the cost of a pot of paint.

44. Giant Charm Bracelet.	**45.** Camp Site.

46. Bronze rams.

Plants are living sculpture, either because of their inherent shape, colour and texture, or because they can be clipped to create a variety of fascinating topiary forms and hedges.

1. *Cycas revolute.*

1 (Previous page) The Japanese sago cycad (*Cycas revolute*) is more cold tolerant than most and a strikingly handsome plant, especially when sporting a brand new crown of leaves.

2 Bromeliads are popular plants because of their good looks and low maintenance requirements. These evergreen, rosette-forming plants are suited to warm climates.

3 Known as the tractor seat ligularia (*Ligularia reniformis*) for its large, glossy green, kidney-shaped leaves, this plant makes an eye-catching statement in lightly shaded areas.

4 Rengarenga or rock lilies (*Arthropodium cirratum*) are versatile plants, happily carpeting the ground in light shade beneath trees. Their strappy leaves form a dense cover, topped by masses of airy little white flowers in early summer.

5 Burgundy *Neoregelia* hybrids provide a strong contrast to the beautifully marked leaves of *Vriesea hieroglyphica* bromeliads and ferns.

Plants can be used as living sculpture in two ways. Some are inherently sculptural because of their shape, colour or texture. Others lend themselves to clipping and shaping to create interesting hedges and topiary forms.

Traditionally associated with formal gardens, the latter approach can work equally well in contemporary gardens. The human instinct for control as a means of survival makes us respond to the strong, clean lines of a formal garden because the sense of order is calming and reassuring. A more relaxed, natural approach can have the same effect, but it is often more difficult to achieve successfully. Lacking boundaries, it can too easily slip into a formless muddle or even downright chaos – never restful.

Bold, dramatic forms, especially upright ones, can make better use of space in a restricted area than loose, flowing patterns can. For example a standard, a shrub or tree trimmed of its lower branches and then allowed to grow into a rounded lollipop shape at the top, will leave room underneath for further planting or paving. Sometimes the same effect is gained by grafting the required cultivar on to strong-growing root stock. Another advantage of standards is that plants that would normally be far too large for a small garden can be easily accommodated. Mop-top robinias, lilly pillies (varieties from Syzygium

3. *Ligularia reniformis.*	**4.** *Arthropodium cirratum.*	**5.** Colourful bromeliads.

6 Happiest by the water, this perennial (*Gunnera manicata*) has leaves like giant platters that make a dramatic impact in the garden.

7 Bromeliads and ferns provide a trouble-free border beneath the canopy offered by tall palms.

8 The felt-like grey leaves of the Persian shield plant (*Strobilanthes gossypinus*) (bottom left) and the blue palm (*Bismarkia nobilis*) (top right) contrast with *Cordyline negra* and the yellow shrimp plant (*Justicia brandegeana lutea*) (bottom right).

9 Heart-shaped, brightly coloured caladiums and snowy impatiens stand out against their greener subtropical counterparts.

and Waterhousea) hollies, bay trees, sprawling roses like 'Sea Foam', the port wine magnolia (*Michelia figo*), camellias, wisteria, Solanum rantonnetii (blue potato bush), corokia, choisya, pyracantha, olives, viburnum, gooseberries and cranberries are all much more manageable when grown in this way. They are expensive to buy because it takes years to train them into impressive specimens but you can easily grow your own – all you need is patience.

Topiary lets you fantasise and play with different shapes and patterns. You might want to repeat rounded shapes that you have used horizontally – to ground-hugging effect – in a vertical treatment. Equally, tall cone shapes can provide a point of contrast to squares and block-like hedges or built elements on a lower level. Using shapes that echo or contrast with other elements in the garden creates a sense of balance and harmony. A circle in the ground pattern will balance a sphere or ball shape in a vertical standard. Mushroom-shaped, clipped box around a semi-circular water feature reinforces the shape. Tall natural cones of thuja can offset or complement wire, bamboo or willow tripods. Spiralling aluminium or steel supports will reinforce koru, snail or nautilus shell shapes used on the ground.

Smaller-leafed plants are best for topiary and it pays to choose those with a growth rate you feel comfortable with. Slower-growing plants such as box, yew and totara will need clipping only once

6. *Gunnera manicata.*	**7.** Subtropical mix.	**8.** Tapestry blend.

9. Poolside glow.

10. Green wall.

11. Groundcover.

12. Foxtail Fern.

10 A stunning combination of bamboo and delicate ferns covers this wall in a Sydney garden.

11 *Elatostema* is a native species of herb that makes a brilliant groundcover in shady moist areas.

12 *Asparagus myersii*, also known as bottle brush fern, has ornamental cylindrical branches of emerald green, making it a desirable houseplant and ideal for hanging baskets.

13 *Muehlenbeckia complexa* shows off its ability to climb on these fantasy figures outside the Ian Potter Foundation Children's Garden at the Royal Botanic Gardens, Melbourne, Australia.

or twice a year, depending on the local climate and conditions. Others such as Lonicera nitida (box honeysuckle) and Solanum species will romp away and you will have to stop them getting out of hand and losing their intended shapes. If you are in a hurry, or daunted by the shaping skills required for topiary, it might be better to buy or make your own basic form out of wire, fleshing it out if necessary with chicken wire. Then you can grow a fast-growing climber like ivy or a creeping fig over the frame.

Instead of an ordinary hedge, consider the English method of pleaching a single row or parallel lines of suitable trees for a 'hedge on stilts' effect. As with standards, the growing trunks are limbed up or trimmed and then the branches at the top are trained along horizontal wires until they mesh together. You end up with a sharp line of straight trunks supporting a solid hedge above. If left bare, the trunks allow you to see through to the rest of the garden, or even a borrowed landscape. Alternatively, you can back the arrangement with a solid fence, painted or stained so that the trunks stand out more clearly. In a tiny garden, a single specimen pleached on either side of the trunk above a solid wall will screen out a neighbouring property entirely. Titoki (*Alectryon excelsus*) and the deciduous northern hemisphere beech, hornbeam and lime or linden are all suitable for this kind of treatment.

13. Imaginary creatures.

⑭ An ephiphytic orchid from Australia, *Dendrobium speciosum*, has found a perfect spot to roost in the branches of an oak tree.

⑮ Rows of *Prunus cerasifera Pissardii* provide a warm welcome in this avenue at the entrance to Quinta Nicolasa, Santiago.

⑯ Especially happy in sandy soils by the beach, *Leucospermum cordifolium* from South Africa makes a great show in spring and summer when its bright orange tubular flowers open.

Cloud topiary is a special form created in the east and based on the same principles as bonsai. The branches of a bushy shrub are thinned out and trimmed where they grow from the main trunk, to reveal the basic structure of the plant. Then the foliage on the end of each branch is clipped into a puffy 'cloud' so that the original shrub takes on the appearance of a small tree. A single specimen can look stunning in a container against the blank canvas of a plain wall, or multiplied in a row for that extra 'wow' factor.

For the ultimate in designer topiary, try growing your standard by twining the stem around a supporting stake. Then remove the stake and you will be left with a twisted or spiralling stem with the standard toadstool or sphere of foliage above. Plaited stems take the challenge a step further as they require a grafting process, and they are much in demand as designer accessories. Ficus benjamina (weeping fig) varieties will respond well to this fashionable treatment.

Traditionally, herb gardens were made easier to manage by enclosing them in box hedges. A parterre is similar but is usually filled with ornamental plants. This method of laying out strongly geometrical shapes on the ground, edging them with low hedges and contrasting fillers or intertwining 'threads' came to be known as the knot garden. It was designed to be looked down on from the terraces and upper

14. Squatter.	**15.** Brilliant avenue.

16. Seaside colour.

17. Olive wall.

18. Orange wall.

19. Glossy cover.

17 The amenable olive tree has been espaliered against a fence, making an attractive screen at a garden café by the sea.

18 *Pyracantha angustifolia* can be clipped to form a dense wall covering, smothered in orange berries in autumn and winter.

19 Frost tender *Tecomanthe speciosa* spreads its large glossy leaves over this wooden wall. When the weather cools in autumn, bunches of creamy white tube-like flowers will add to the display.

20 A well-kept variation on the topiary theme makes for an attractive wall.

21 Different sizes of immaculately clipped box balls demonstrate the visual power exerted by the formal garden.

windows of a large house. Today, these ideas are back in vogue for the simple reason that they work well in confined spaces. Mediterranean plants such as teucrium, santolina, rosemary and lavender all respond to clipping and have proved reliable over the years. With fresh combinations and innovative use of these and other malleable plants (besides that old stalwart, box, or one of its substitutes), we can reinvent a medieval art-form for the twenty-first century.

The French are credited with the age-old custom of espalier, whereby fruit trees are trained along wires so they can be kept flat against a wall or on the sides of a tunnelled archway. Pears and apples are popular subjects, illustrating again that these control mechanisms make large trees quite feasible in a small patch. If evergreen foliage is required, camellias also respond well to such treatment.

If you prefer your plants to grow naturally or you know that you will never keep on top of a clipping regime, choose plants with naturally strong shapes. Smaller-growing hebes, for example, will grow into rounded humps without any assistance. Planted in strong groups, they give the garden a definite outline,

20. Topiary wall.	**21.** Box balls.

22 The famous garden at Levens Hall, near Kendal in the UK, has some of the oldest topiary in the world.

23 The devoted attention of generations of gardeners has resulted in these meticulously sculpted topiary forms also at Levens Hall.

24 An ornamental climber adds a painterly splash of red to these clipped yews at York Gate Garden in Leeds.

25 An outstanding example of trees clipped into a traditional style of topiary known as cloud-pruning.

resembling an outcrop of boulders or a flock of woolly sheep lying down in the shade of a tree, or even plants sculpted by on-shore winds near the coast. Conifers like cypresses and thujas can form majestic conical or cylindrical hedges – all you have to do is plant them side by side, allowing sufficient space for their mature forms. Japanese maples (*Acer palmatum*) are naturally compact and have delicate, ferny foliage and brilliant autumn colour. The Dissectum group maples have especially fine filigree leaves of bright green or dark purple. In winter, the tracery of their bare branches is also attractive.

If there is no room for the trees you remember with nostalgia from your parents' or grandparents' gardens, find out if there is a fastigiate (upright) form. A copper beech may be out of the question in a city garden, but the cultivar *Fagus sylvatica* 'Dawyck Purple' will squeeze into a confined space because it grows vertically instead of developing into an enormous, spreading giant, more suitable for a park. The tulip tree, *Liriodendron tulipifera* 'Fastigiatum', with its chopped off leaves and fabulous autumn colour, is another example. And don't forget that amazing living fossil, the ginkgo (*Ginkgo biloba*) or maidenhair tree. Its unusual fan-shaped leaves turn pure yellow in autumn and yes, there is a columnar form – 'Fastigiata', which will grow to a mere 10 m straight up instead of 25 m with a 10 m girth.

Some plants ooze sculptural form in a dramatic fashion. The ancient cycad is spell-binding all

22. Golden afternoon.	**23.** Ancient splendour.	**24.** Red splash.

25. Cloud trees.

26. Knot Garden.

26 Variegated pyramids of buxus stand out against the plain green hedges of the Knot Garden at Bourton House, Gloucestershire.

27 Teucrium clipped into flowing forms is brought into sharp relief by the vivid iresine surrounding the plant support in this Auckland garden by Trish Bartleet.

28 Sculpted from yew trees, these grand corpulent chessmen decorate the Christchurch garden of retired architect Sir Miles Warren.

29 Green-on-green formality, edged with black mondo echoing the pebbles in the paving, works in flawless harmony in a garden by Eckersley Stafford Design, Melbourne.

27. Silver waves.

28. Let's play.

29. Squiggly hedge.

30 Slow to flower and fruit, the berries of the Kermadec nikau (*Rhopalostylis baueri* var. *cheesemanii*) are worth the wait.

31 *Bismarkia nobilis*, the Bismark or blue palm, has amazing sculptural form and the colour of its leaves make it stand out in front of a nikau and *Washingtonia filifera*, the cotton or desert palm.

32 Towering palm trees are balanced by a substantial flight of grass-topped steps in pleasing proportions at the Quillota Garden, designed by Juan Grimm, Chile.

33 Young nikau palms show off their fine shuttlecock form above *Muehlenbeckia astonii* and *Fuchsia procumbens* in a Herne Bay garden designed by Trish Bartleet.

34 Australian grass trees (*Xanthorrhoea australis*), bear magnificent heads of the finest of leaves on stout trunks. Their other nickname is 'black boy' because their trunks are often blackened, but still living, after being burned in bush fires.

on its own – a group is seriously impressive. Agaves and dracaenas are other groups that demand attention because of their bold, sharp forms that need no treatment aside from discerning placement. Sempervivums and aeoniums have perfectly shaped rosettes of typically fleshy succulent leaves to attract attention. Aeonium arboretum 'Schwarzkopf' (a tree aeonium) has riveting dark purple-black colouring to boot.

Subtropical plants rely on the fiery flamboyance of their remarkable foliage for dramatic impact. Bromeliads, especially the larger alcantareas, pack a huge punch in terms of both colour and shape with their bold, stiffly pointed or arching leaves. Some also have fascinating markings. Coleus, crotons, caladiums and iresines have vividly jewel-like foliage that makes for glittering groundcover. The paintbrush flower, scadoxus, is a tender bulb whose bright scarlet or soft yellow globes light up the shade under trees like Chinese lanterns.

Feathery grasses like Chionochloa and gossamer grass (*Anemanthele lessoniana*) rely more on texture than shape and can be arrestingly effective en masse. Trees that have a similar effect include the jacaranda and the silk tree (*Albizia julibrissin*). The foliage of the fern community is inherently beautiful

30. Nikau berries.	**31.** Palm trees.

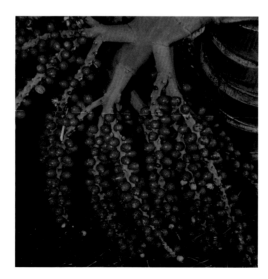 

32. Perfect balance.

33. Fine form.

34. Grass trees.

35. Leaf patterns.

36. *Aloe polyphylla.*

37. *Aloe plicatilis.*

35 *Yucca elephantipes, Aloe thraskii* and agapanthus are a sound recipe for a low-maintenance garden where water is in short supply.

36 The spiral aloe (*Aloe polyphylla*) has such perfection of form that it cannot fail to impress. Unlike other aloes, it needs water and can cope with cold as it is from the mountain areas in Lesotho, which are often covered in snow.

37 The fan aloe (*Aloe plicatilis*) has leaves on one plane and a well-branched specimen, full of 'fans', is a fascinating sight as it is capable of growing up to 5 m.

38 Designer, Juan Grimm often uses a Chilean native plant Chagualillo (*Puya venusta*) because of its attractively dense silvery rosettes of spiny-edged leaves and striking reddish-violet flowers.

and the taller-growing tree-ferns towering out of the mist can resemble a forest from ages past. They are all moisture-loving bush- or forest-dwellers by nature and will need shelter and plenty of water to give of their best in a garden situation. We have all been snared by the exquisite finery of the maidenhair fern as an indoor pot plant at some time or other, only to find that even daily misting is not quite enough to keep them in perfect condition.

Palms vary in height but all share the characteristics of a striking evergreen leafy crown on a clear stem. The shape of their leaves – either feather-shaped (pinnate) or fan-shaped (palmate) – makes them a stunning addition to any garden. Perfect for narrow, shady beds at the sides of a house or for providing a canopy of shade, they also grow well in containers. This makes them ideal for both indoors and outdoors, blurring the distinction between the two.

Water plants or those with an affinity for boggy marshland at the edges of ponds and lakes are a great source of bold shape. Gunneras have the edge here and with their enormous jagged and deeply lobed leaves they need careful siting or they can completely take over and obscure the water from view. For subtropical gardens, two food crops from the tropics have magnificently large, lush, arrow-shaped

38. *Puya venusta.*

39. The Huntington.

39 Golden barrel cacti (*Echinocactus grusonii*) make a splash of yellow in the Desert Garden at The Huntington, San Marino, California, which has one of the oldest and largest collections of cacti and other succulents in the world. The dark-leaved plant in the foreground is a bromeliad hybrid called Dyckia or Eight Ball.

40 A trio of *Agave* aff. *franzosinii*, with golden barrel cacti beyond, in the 10-acre cacti and succulent garden at The Huntington.

41 Known as the dune aloe (*Aloe thraskii*), its sunny yellow flowers will brighten up the garden in winter.

42 A range of aloes thrives in this colourful border at Totara Waters Subtropical Garden in Whenuapai, Auckland.

40. Desert Garden.

41. *Aloe thraskii.*

42. Aloe border.

Philodendron Xanadu finishes off this double-barrelled hedge of *Hymenosporum flavum* Gold Nugget, a small growing version of the Australian frangipani tree, and *Griselinia littoralis*.

The columnar form of towering cereus cacti reinforce the light columns at the entrance to this rural property.

A giant *Agave Americana* Variegata issues a spiny welcome at the entrance to a suitably 'hot' looking sleep-out in Newtown, Wellington.

leaves and both will thrive in wet areas: taro (*Colocasia esculenta*) and the more tender yautia or tannia (*Xanthosoma sagittifolium*).

Many plants with velvety grey or silver leaves are strong on texture and some also boast a striking form and felt-like leaves. Globe artichokes and their cousins the cardoons (*Cynara cardunculus*) have arching silver-grey leaves that zoom skywards to 2.5 m, with the added bonus of purple-mauve, thistle-like flower heads on top. Stachys byzantina 'Silver Carpet' (lambs' ears) is a favourite as a border plant for its woolly, grey-green leaves, and the taller variety 'Big Ears' will give a bit of height further back in the border.

Red and purple foliage will always stand out in a sea of green and is well worth exploring. One variety of the Judas tree, Cercis canadensis 'Forest Pansy', has deep reddish-purple leaves that first emerge as glowing red hearts before deepening in tone. Cotinus coggygria 'Royal Purple', a form of the smoke bush, also has dark purple leaves changing to scarlet in autumn. Purple akeake or Dodonaea viscosa 'Purpurea' is a popular light hedging plant with purple foliage and a purple tinge to its flowers and seed capsules too. Flaxes (phormiums) and cabbage trees (cordylines) are available in an ever increasing

43. Plant Patterns.

44. Cacti garden.

45. Mexico meets Wellington.

46. Clifftop boardwalk.

46 Access to the far corners of this garden, Tiromoana at Okitu in Poverty Bay, is made easy with a solid boardwalk meandering among clumps of flaxes bending gracefully in the offshore wind.

47 A wiry, divaricating brown hedge of *Coprosma virescens* is cleverly offset by the sword-like green leaves of the Poor Knights lily (*Xeronema callistemon*).

48 *Aloe thraskii*, the dune aloe, combines happily with native toetoe and flax in dry, sandy conditions on the coast at Kuaotunu on the Coromandel Peninsula.

range of colourful varieties, and a trip to your local plant nursery to see what is on offer is bound to pay dividends.

The sword-like leaves of flaxes or phormiums, astelias, xeronemas (Poor Knights lilies) and arthropodiums are favourites for making a big impact, especially in large groups. Cabbage trees do the same thing at a greater height. Ligularias, on the other hand, have huge kidney-shaped leaves for contrasting form.

Still other plants have weird juvenile forms. Lancewoods such as Pseudopanax crassifolius and the even stranger saw-toothed P. ferox have rod-like stems, with downward-pointing spoke-like branches

47. Colour and texture.	**48.** Coastal plants.

49 Rusty brown carex species give movement and light to the garden when rustled by the wind.

50 Aureola or golden Japanese forest grass (*Hakonechloa macra*) is a graceful, flowing plant that can look like a golden waterfall when under full sun. It is also ideal for lightening up a shady corner.

51 A powerful arrangement of clumping mondo grass leads the eye straight to the water feature bordered by a pair of *Lepidozamia peroffskyana* at the end of this subtropical courtyard, edged with gardenias and ginger plants.

from the top. Slow growers, they will eventually grow into more regular tree forms. Ribbonwood (*Plagianthus regius*) has a fascinatingly wiry juvenile stage before developing into a mature tree with leaves not unlike those of a silver birch.

The pale trunks of eucalyptus and silver birches create a ghostly effect when planted close together in groups or parallel lines, as in the traditional rows either side of a long driveway. The cultivar *Betula utilis* var. *jacquemontii* (West Himalayan birch) has such distinctively beautiful white bark that it needs no more than a single specimen to create a lasting impression. Try growing a group of naturally slender trees like these, or the remarkable mountain or Chinese tallow tree, *Sapium discolor* or *sebiferum*, in an outdoor living area with just the bare minimum of seating: you will enjoy the delicate, airy experience of the light shade they cast. Frost-tender tallow trees have the added benefit of brilliant red leaves that cling to the trees in autumn.

Visualise the picture you are trying to paint with your garden, and then seek out the plants that will give you the three-dimensional sculptural effect that you want to create colour, texture and form.

49. Native grasses.

50. Golden grass.

If you want atmosphere in the garden, explore the possibilities of including water. From the tiniest water feature to a lake, nothing else captures that sense of peace and refreshment.

water

2. Fantasia.

1 (Previous page) Outsize pieces of a puzzle depicting Botticelli's *The Birth of Venus* float about on the pond in a garden which explores the possibilities of play at the Chaumont-sur-Loire Garden Festival, 2006.

2 Head gardener Stuart Ferries of Eden Garden, Epsom, came up with a crowd pleaser when he designed these large clear water cylinders (complete with goldfish) for an award-winning, jungle-inspired garden at the Ellerslie Flower Show, 2006.

3 By combining elements unique to New Zealand, such as the koru-shaped stainless steel and glass water feature and woven nikau panels, designer Ben Hoyle has created a distinctive garden for today's Kiwi lifestyle.

4 Careful selection and placement of Kaiaua river stones was central to the success of this water feature. It was designed by Trish Bartleet for a small entrance courtyard in an inner city garden.

Since ancient times, water has been revered for the magical qualities it brings to a garden. The source of life, it irrigates and refreshes, soothes and restores, cools and tranquillises. In short, there is nothing to match it for introducing a particular tone, establishing a special atmosphere – that elusive 'mood' that all gardeners yearn for.

Maintenance puts a lot of people off the idea of including water in their gardens and that objection is perfectly valid. Water is not the straightforward affair that pool providing companies and water feature outlets would have you believe. But it is almost always worth the effort, and if you do your homework and find out what will suit you and what you will be able to manage, then don't hesitate to go ahead because it will give you endless pleasure. Climate can be a big factor. If you live in a temperate zone without major fluctuations you won't have to worry about the effect of severe frosts, which can wreak havoc with pipes, pumps and ceramic bowls and containers.

Swimming pools require expert advice and design. The style of pool should suit your house and your

3. Contemporary Kiwi.	**4.** River stones.

5 Designed by Jamie Durie of PATIO Landscape Architecture and Design, this water feature has water sweeping around its weathered steel wall, accentuating its curved shape and embracing the pond and feathery plants within.

6 Water falling from a reflective stainless steel 'ribbon' into a pool adds vitality to this Chelsea show garden celebrating life and the beauty of nature, created for Cancer Research UK, 2004.

7 A simple jet fountain brings this gentle water feature, designed by Out from the Blue, Melbourne, to life, with its water lilies and other aquatic plants providing a haven for resident fish.

needs: a contemporary home deserves a pool to complement its architecture while a more traditional or classical style will look more in keeping in the grounds of an older colonial Victorian or Edwardian house. Depending on the depth of your pocket, you can hand over the management completely or partially or do it all yourself. The company that installs the pool will usually offer you these options and get you up and running at the very least, with the ongoing offer of full service should you be away from home for any length of time, or be unable to look after your pool because of ill health or other commitments.

To get the right effect with water anywhere in your property, think carefully about the sound you want a water feature to make. Do you prefer a soft, soothing, tinkling or bubbling effect or would you rather have a more dramatic waterfall plunging into the reservoir below? The latter can be useful for drowning out street or traffic noise and is definitely more exciting, but equally it can easily become too loud and harsh for comfort – even torturous if placed near a living area. The net result will be that you turn it off instead of enjoying it.

5. Water wall.

6. Life Garden.

7. Goldfish pool.

8. Japanese influence.

8 A bamboo water spout proves the maxim that less is more by adding just the right amount of sound and visual interest to this quiet glade.

9 Wall-mounted water spouts are the best option if space is limited and they can take a variety of forms to suit different tastes.

10 Atmosphere is the key to a successful grotto; a melancholy air of mystery is a key element.

11 Surrounded by soft planting, this lion's head disgorges water straight into the tranquil blue-green water of the swimming pool at Quinta Nicolasa, Chile.

9. Lion's head.

10. Grotto.

11. Downward head.

12 An oriental pot and wafting papyrus plant add an exotic touch to the pool in this tiny courtyard.

13 Water as the central vital feature in a desert garden is given a bold contemporary twist in this minimalist interpretation.

14 The movement of water creates a magical experience on many levels in this Oratia garden.

As water always acts like a magnet, young children must be kept safe from it at all times. A simple bubble fountain splashing gently over smooth rocks is generally the safest option as there is no depth to worry about.

Even the tiniest garden can have water in some form. The simplest approach is a pot or container, with water flowing over the edges and spilling smoothly down the sides. For example a glazed Vietnamese pot, set upon a basic plastic tray that is hidden under a layer of pebbles, can be most effective. The water then drains down into a trough containing a small pump that sends it back up again to the top of the main container. This is perfect for small balconies as it doesn't splash and won't make

12. Giant pot.   **13.** Oasis.

14. Brimming cauldron.

15. Mahuhu Ki Te Rangi Reserve.

15 Landscape designer Ted Smyth created this tranquil, contemporary water sculpture at Mahuhu Ki Te Rangi Reserve, Quay Park, Auckland, using Maori motifs to reflect its return to the ownership of Ngati Whatua.

16 A colourful tiled rill trickling down a stepped hillside evokes images of ancient gardens in hot lands where water was revered for its cooling, spiritual and life-giving properties.

17 In this contemporary design Jamie Durie has created a generous rill, stepping down towards the sea, embellished with soft, moss-like plants.

a huge noise. Also it is easy to keep clean with a bromide tablet, as used in spa pools. Choose a colour to go with your interior scheme, sit back and enjoy your very own feature just outside your door.

Possibly even less space is required for a vertical element: a mounted water spout or a sheet of water sliding down a wall of stainless steel or other treated metal. Glass too can be especially dramatic as a backdrop. Different effects can be obtained if the surface is etched or patterned, and lights can transform it at night. The water supply should be hidden behind or within the wall when it is being built.

If you have a little more room, an ornamental pool will lend itself to a range of different treatments. You might want to consider filling it with plants and fish, although both will bake in full sun if the pool is really small. In that case, opt for a clean, uncluttered look and keep the mosquitoes at bay with a chemical and algae solution. Inanimate ornaments made of glass or stone will draw the eye, or you might include a small bubble fountain. A small pump is all that is needed to create movement and subtle sound.

16. Stepped rill.	**17.** Wide rill.

18 The chiselled-glass rill and laminated glass pond in Xanthe White's award-winning entry at the Chelsea Flower Show, 2006, shows what a captivating combination glass and water can be in the garden.

19 Sculptor Virginia King created the skeletal stainless steel lacebark leaf floating on the large dark reflective pond. The overall design was inspired by the unique nature of Auckland's west coast beaches.

20 A long rill leading to a large pond is part of a highly symmetrical layout, designed by Andrew Pfeiffer to echo the plant forms in this surprising desert garden.

Clear glass bricks are great for constructing such a pool above ground. Alternatively, you can use black tiles or a darkly tinted plaster finish on a still pool to enhance its reflective qualities, although it can be disconcerting if it's so dark you can't see what's in it.

Fountains have a long tradition in the public realm of city parks and gardens so they tend to come with an image of formality and grandeur. They are certainly powerful focal points so it is essential that they are in proportion to their overall surroundings. Like any other strong feature, they will make you stop and enjoy the spectacle before moving on to look at the rest of the garden: bear that in mind if you want to insert a pause or break a long line in the garden, before continuing to another viewpoint. One of the most attractive ways of using fountains is to multiply them and reduce them in size to small bubble fountains, usually in a row at the edge of a larger pool, possibly marking the transition from one part to another. The effect is soft and gentle and utterly irresistible.

18. 100% Pure NZ.	**19.** Lacebark leaf.

㉑ House and garden merge on this property so that the Denis O'Connor sculpture, *Bird Call*, with its oar reflected in the pool, appears to be virtually inside the living room.

㉒ Landscape designer Rod Barnett has created a sail of water above the endless blue of the Waitemata Harbour at Takapuna, Auckland.

㉓ A summer-house, graced with white swans, is reflected in the still waters of a pair of lakes in this large garden at Coatesville, north of Auckland.

㉔ Water gushing from a crevice between two large rocks makes a simple but enlivening waterfall for this swimming pool in St Mary's Bay, Auckland.

Watching the birds dipping their wings and splashing about in a birdbath is one of the most affordable pleasures of gardening. All you have to do is keep it fresh and clean for them. Sculptors and craftspeople are constantly coming up with original versions but you can also think outside the square and find or make something that works for you. Take some care to place it where you will be able to see it but not so close that the birds will be frightened off at the slightest sound. Don't forget to put it out of easy reach of the neighbourhood cats.

Water rills – narrow little channels set in the ground to carry water from one area to another – are endlessly fascinating. In Islamic gardens they were laid out in a cross to indicate the four quarters of the universe. At the centre, the channels always converged on a fountain or pool, symbolising the spring of life. Equally symbolic plantings were used to soften the strictly geometric layout of these rectangular gardens. Fortunately, they were also inherently practical, as the flowing water cooled the desert air, while the fruit trees and palms provided both nourishment and refreshment.

On a sloping site, rills are traditionally stepped down at intervals to follow the contours of the land, taking on a life of their own and usually culminating in a pool at the bottom or lowest level. The water

21. Water sculpture.

22. Water on water.

23. Twin Lakes.

24. Rock waterfall.

25. Papudo.

25 The still water of the swimming pool mirrors exactly the colour of the far more turbulent sea off the rocky coast of Chile, emphasising the division between cultivated garden and wild landscape.

26 The gentle ripples caused by sculptor Roderick Burgess's nikau water feature barely affect the reflection of the trees in this dark pool, designed by Gudrun Fischer to be both ornamental and recreational.

27 Designer John Patrick has managed to seamlessly merge a new spa and swimming pool into the garden of an older style home in Toorak, Melbourne.

is then pumped up again out of sight beneath the ground to create a constant flow. Even a single rill beside the path leading to a front door can be worthwhile, especially if the stones or tiles in the bottom are chosen with care. Think back to those special stone collections of childhood, when even the dullest object would take on a fresh new glow and vividness of colour when it was underwater.

Moving water of any kind in the garden will pull you towards its source and so is an excellent way of drawing people through or down into areas where they might not be tempted to go if that magnetic force was not present. It can also soften a severely formal design, making it much more palatable, especially as any movement comes with the extra bonus of a soft sound. You can use it to link various parts of the garden and act as a unifying element. Some rills, for example, run right through the house before emerging in the garden. Occasionally small streams are designed like this too, emerging underground in the lower levels of the house, although you have to be able to turn them off as the sound is a constant factor.

26. Green pool. **27.** City pool.

28 A large lake lends itself to the beauty of waterlilies, with their flat green pads and the startlingly clear colours of their star-like blooms.

29 High on the hill at Driving Creek Potteries and Railway, near Coromandel, is this charming pool nestled in the bush and overlooking the coast.

30 Landscape designer Juan Grimm developed his own personal haven in this stunning location overlooking the Pacific Ocean, at Bahia Azul on the coast of Chile.

Natural pools and waterfalls are capable of transporting us straight into the bush or forest, instantly weaving the magic of a mountain stream in our own back yard. Once the rock formation has been completed to get the required look, the waterfall can be operated by a single pump to maintain the illusion. The pool will need to have a thick butyl rubber or plastic liner and the edges must then be concealed by plants or carefully placed stones. This initial work is often better left to the experts as leakage is a common problem. In an urban environment such features are better as part of an informal garden, preferably with a reasonable amount of space, so that they don't look too contrived and out of place.

In the country, an informal pool can expand to become a pond or even a lake, sometimes a whole series of them. Water on this scale can become addictive and it is not hard to see why. Lakes can be planted with a wonderful variety of trees and water-loving plants such as the magnificent Japanese

28. Waterlilies.	**29.** Rocky pool.

30. Circular haven.

31. Connecting lakes.

31 Vast serpentine stone walls create extensive lakes of dammed water that flow into each other as they step majestically down the hill at Chiñihue Garden, Melipilla, Chile.

32 The brilliant autumn tones of *Nyssa sylvatica* and *Quercus palustris* (right) trees make an impressive sight around a pond at Flaxmere, a rural garden in North Canterbury.

33 Perfectly still water in a circular pond and a long directional canal are sheltered and defined by the use of tightly clipped totara hedges in a garden designed by Robert Watson at Broadfields, near Christchurch on the Canterbury Plains.

irises. They become a haven for all manner of birds, fish and wildlife; to say nothing of the hours of fun to be had floating about on them in rafts, kayaks and rowing boats.

Perhaps the most romantic companion for water in a garden is a floating deck, boardwalk or other contemporary variation on the moat of old. Nothing beats looking out on a tranquil waterscape from the comfort of your own living area, or a part of the garden. Such large-scale ponds and lakes are only possible in the country or where there is plenty of space but shallow, confined versions can also be incorporated sleekly into city gardens with stunning results. In fact, some of the most beautiful gardens in the world would be nothing without this superlative treatment.

Plants are important in a water garden as the more leaf cover you have, the cleaner the water will be. If you add a few fish they will eat most of the inevitable mosquito larvae and will also appreciate the protection provided by the leaves from marauding cats and birds. Frogs and tadpoles are desirable additions too, although if the fish are big enough they might eat the tadpoles or, alternatively, the frogs might eat your small fish. You need to get the sizes in proportion; otherwise let nature sort out the victors

32. Flaxmere.

33. Reflections.

34 This large angular rock sculpture by Graham Mumford looks as if it might have been dropped from the sky to settle into a water lily pool in Mt Eden, Auckland.

35 A large floating circle of red-painted corrugated iron by sculptor John Haines has the effect of focusing the eye and framing the reflections of giant taro leaves on the far side of this pond.

36 A pair of stainless steel dragonflies by sculptor Virginia King hover over a natural-looking pond bursting with subtropical water plants in Mt Eden, Auckland.

or a workable balance. There are numerous variations on the goldfish theme, both in colour and shape, so take your pick. Remember though, that fish will thrive in a larger pool, where the surface area will help absorb oxygen. It also needs to be deep enough – at least 450 mm so that it won't get too hot in the summer.

Far from the simple oxygen weed of the past, there is now a huge array of suitable plant material for water gardens. Basically there are three categories: water lilies, submerged plants and marginal or bog plants. Remember that the more plants you have, the better your fish will like it.

Monet's water lily paintings based on his garden at Giverny have done much to spread the popularity of these beautiful plants. There are two kinds – hardy and tropical, differing from each other less in climatic preferences than in growth and flowering habits. The hardy varieties don't flower as vigorously but are useful for their winter leaves. Tropical water lilies can have up to 75 per cent more flowers and these will appear all summer long.

34. Block sculpture.

35. Corrugated iron.

36. Dragonflies.

37. Stepping stones.

38. Natural pool.

39. Stony stream.

37 Frangipani-patterned stepping stones make a fitting path across a pool full of tropical water lilies and water hyacinths in a garden near Ubud, Bali.

38 Surrounded by rocks and partially covered with moss-like plants, this pool by Isabelle Greene blends into the garden landscape without a ripple.

39 Designer Patrick Corfe has chosen to display vibrant day lilies along a clear pebble stream in this Ellerslie Flower Show garden. Large architectural tree ferns add substance and help to balance the built structures.

40 Designed by the owner Patricio Cummins, this beautifully proportioned pool blends into the garden surrounding his traditional residence, Quinta Nicolasa, in Santiago, as if it had been there for ever.

On another level again, the sacred lotus is irresistible, its perfumed flowers softly tinged with pink or pale creamy yellow rising from giant discs of coolest green. As it is an extremely rampant grower, the answer is to contain one in a barrel or other large waterproof pot. After the flowers you will have the bonus of the pods – much prized for flower arrangements.

The best way to get ideas for both plants and construction is to visit your local water garden supplier, garden shows and open gardens, or research the options on the internet and at your library. Landscape designers and contractors will be able to offer any number of suggestions and solutions if you decide to seek professional help.

Swimming pools are not just a practical way of cooling off, having fun or getting valuable exercise – except for lap pools which can be squeezed into the most unlikely spaces at the side of a house or on the boundary of a section. Whatever their size, pools are a dominant architectural addition to the landscape. Bearing in mind that they will be out of use for several months over winter in most countries of the world, it is vital that they don't become depressing eyesores in full view from your main windows. Why not seize the opportunity to turn your pool into an object of beauty? Its singular strength lies in

40. Timeless pool.

41 Inverted bell-shaped pots make wonderful water features for a small corner, providing visual focus and the soft murmuring sound of a bubble fountain, like this one in Neutral Bay, Sydney.

42 There is nothing like an old stone water trough to add an air of venerable age to a garden, as this one does placed at the end of a path leading to the doorway of a home in Nurse Hill, Waimauku.

43 By sinking this formal pool, the owners have made it easy for visitors to enjoy the beautiful sight of the Japanese irises in flower. Controlled water lilies continue the display.

its enormous reflective qualities, so you should make the most of them. A dark pool will become a mirror image of everything around and above it: trees, shrubs, clouds and sky. For year-round interest, you can always include a water feature as part of the overall design.

Most importantly, swimming pools need to sit well in their environment – easily achieved in a contemporary urban setting where they essentially merge with the architecture of the dwelling. In the country or by the sea, a lake or a river, where magnificent natural scenery dominates, this is much more difficult to achieve in a pleasing, harmonious way. Infinity pools may provide the ideal solution but equally it can sometimes be better not to try and compete. Instead, simply place such artifice to one side and allow nature to reign supreme.

If exercise is important and you only have room for a plunge pool there is always the option of adding a strong jet to swim against.

Both swimming pools and ornamental pools can benefit from being raised above the ground to

41. Bell jar.	**42.** Stone trough.

43. Sunken pool.

44. Water altar.

45. Zen.

46. Flower.

44 German-born sculptor Rudi Jass, from Melbourne, made this free-flowing stainless steel and stone water feature. Its clean lines complement the pool perfectly.

45 A wall-mounted water feature by Rudi Jass is reminiscent of a Japanese tea ceremony, consisting simply of a bronze jug pouring water into a stainless steel bowl sitting on a bed of stones.

46 In this variation on a theme, Rudi Jass has created a blue glass 'flower' bowl, fed by a stainless steel water spout on either side.

47 Sculptor Rick Rudd made this intriguing water feature of a Japanese-style pot pouring water into a tea cup for the courtyard beside his house in Castlecliff, Wanganui.

48 A stainless steel and glass cross over design by Rudi Jass makes a fresh focal point in a modern courtyard.

provide a broad perimeter ledge for extra seating. This also has the advantage of making them difficult for a small child or pet to enter.

Spa pools or hot tubs are a much cheaper option than a swimming pool and may suit your purposes better. They are a wonderful way to relax and ease aching joints, and children love them. Best of all, they fit into a tiny space – even a deck can often accommodate one. You can enjoy the sight of the stars above if your tub is open to the night sky or you can cover a basic pergola to protect bathers from heavy rain. Better still, use a clear material for the roof and then you will have the best of both worlds.

Apart from style and placement, colour is one of the most important decisions you will have to make about a swimming pool. As it is a permanent, artificial feature, it is generally wiser to go for a darker, more natural-looking tone that will be easy to live with year-round. In the dead of winter you don't want to look out on an abandoned Pacific Island resort. That said, exciting colour treatments in confident hands can certainly turn a pool into a work of art.

| **47.** Japanese tea pot. | **48.** Glass dishes. |

Pots are the easiest way to add a decorative element to any garden. From an apartment to a stately home, they can provide a focal point, drama, colour and interest.

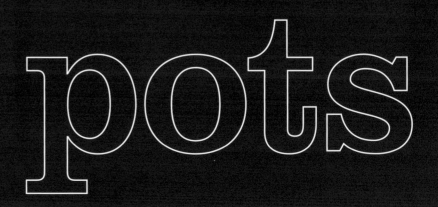

1. Flat bowl.

2. Wooden barrel.

1 (Previous page) The Poor Knight's Lily (*Xeronema callistemon*) prefers having its roots severely restricted, making this flat terracotta bowl the ideal container.

2 With a coat of paint, a barrel made of half rounds of timber becomes a fine container for a rare citrus plant, Buddha's Hand citron (*Citrus medica* var. *sarcodactylus*), a symbol of supreme happiness.

3 Sandstone pots painted a rich red contrast perfectly with green foliage plants such as these nikau, alcantareas and spider grass.

4 Decorative ceramic jugs and bowls can be used to accent colours or particular plants in the garden, helping to make them a feature.

Many people begin their gardening lives with a pot or two to cheer up a dingy flat or sterile apartment. Even the least green-thumbed among us will get desperate for some contact with nature when we are severely deprived of it. That's the cue to go out and buy that zappy designer pot, or forage the markets for cheap imports and potters' seconds. Best of all, you can become a craftsperson in your own right. A can of paint and a simple container of terracotta, tin, wood or plastic are all you need to get started. If you don't fancy that approach, you can unleash your creativity on the planting side of the equation.

Imagine the world's cities without pot plants brightening drab brick walls and dull entrances. When imaginative local authorities run competitions for the best-presented railway stations, the most lacklustre are often completely transformed by a few generous containers full of plants. What better

3. Red pots.	**4.** Jug and bowl.

5 Whitewashed pots with topiary spirals of box become living sculpture when placed together in a corner of the garden.

6 For a smart, sleek, sophisticated look you can't go past wooden Versailles tubs painted in a shiny black enamel finish and topped with sculpted topiary emerging from strappy foliage.

7 This traditional knot garden of clipped box hedges has been given a stylish contemporary twist by the addition of a Versailles tub painted a clear bright blue and filled, unexpectedly, with a succulent *Aloe bainesii.*

way to give workers a lift than making sure they are greeted by pots of cheerful colour, offset by calming green, as they face the stress and grind of the daily commute?

Pots lend themselves to every possible area of gardening. They can be used as anchors and focal points in large, rambling country gardens or they can provide the perfect solution for smaller decks and verandahs. In tiny spaces, they may be the only option, lining narrow paths or the edges of pools with the versatility and manoeuvrability that make them so popular. At the front door, there is nothing more welcoming than a bright container boasting spring bulbs, a smartly clipped piece of topiary, or heady perfume. Best of all, pots are totally adaptable. Whether you want to brighten up a dull, shady corner or cool down an area exposed to relentless heat from the sun, there will be a suitable plant you can use. You can make the planting as permanent or as seasonal as you wish. The beauty of the container is that it will remain the same whatever you decide to grow in it – or even if you leave it unplanted. If blue is your favourite flower colour in the garden, for example, you might purchase a large blue pot or paint it the exact shade you prefer, and then settle it in your flower bed. When the plants are in flower, it will echo them and when they are over, it will still be providing you with that special touch of the sky or sea,

5. Topiary spirals.	**6.** Black tubs.

7. Blue tub.

8. Oriental pot.

8 A single, large, oriental pot filled with reeds and water lilies makes an excellent water feature in this private courtyard.

9 A striped ceramic pot by Phillip Luxton makes a powerful statement by breaking up areas of planting and providing focus at Tiromoana, Gisborne.

10 A finely crafted pot will enhance any area, drawing the eye and lifting key colours in walls and furnishings.

11 Enormous terracotta pots at Lo Fontecilla in Santiago, Chile, speak of ages past when such containers were used for storing everyday basic food items such as olive oil.

9. Sculpted pot.

10. Pedestal pot.

11. Giant pots.

12. Dragon pot.

13. Centrepiece.

14. Designer urns.

12 Bathed in light, an *Aloe plicatilis* shows off its perfect fan shape in a large pot adorned with a dragon lizard.

13 A beautifully crafted pot like this tall one by Phillip Luxton makes an ideal courtyard centrepiece.

14 Sculptor Phillip Luxton's concern for form lifts these urns beyond craft into the realm of art.

15 Master craftsman Barry Brickell created this shapely pot, decorated by Samoan-born artist and sculptor Fatu Feu'u.

16 These giant (1.5 m) pots by Phil Neary are made of wood, textured with hammer marks and stained in rich, glowing colours.

campanula, cornflower or delphinium. Pots are easily transportable unless they are huge, and even then you can do it with special trolleys on wheels. If your favourite plants have a high and a low season, trot them out to show off when they are looking their best and whip them away out of sight as soon as they begin to fade. Then simply fill the gap with something else that has been waiting in the wings for its moment on the stage.

The hardest part of container gardening is choosing from the many options available. As with every other part of your decorating, trust your instincts and have some fun experimenting. Sometimes you have to live in places that you can't adapt to suit your own personal taste. Pots allow you to improve that situation dramatically; it's up to you to make the most of it. Prices vary enormously but there is something for everyone, from designer and antique models to simple terracotta pots. In fact terracotta, literally 'baked or fired earth', covers the entire spectrum, from ancient Greek styles to humble everyday nursery pots. Its rustic simplicity and empathy with nature makes it hard to beat. The only downside is that terracotta is too porous for very hot climates, unless you seal it and grow plants that relish desert life.

15. Decorated pot.	**16.** Amphorae.

17 By raising it on a box pedestal, the owner of this elegant piece has highlighted its decorative qualities.

18 Myfanwy Rees designed this simple inverted cone-shaped pot, embellished with a curving koru symbol.

19 Made from Welsh slate by sculptor Howard Bowcott, this shapely vessel has settled comfortably into the Hannah Peschar Sculpture Garden in Surrey.

20 David Carson has perfected the challenging art of weaving discarded saw blades into new sculptural forms, taking recycling to fresh heights.

Traditionally, terracotta pots were used to store food and drink in the countries bordering the Mediterranean: this proved especially useful for keeping liquids cool in summer. Such containers would also have kept flour, grains and other food safe from foraging animals. Original versions range from simple yoghurt pots to large olive oil urns and a variety of amphora, or two-handled pots, often used for transporting goods from place to place – frequently by sea. Old or antique pots have a patina that comes with age and makes them look at home in any garden, without the need for plant life to further adorn them. You can cheat with brand-new pots by smearing them with yoghurt to encourage the growth of lichen and moss. Liquid seaweed manure can be painted on for an instant maturing effect as well.

If you want to add your own personal touch or bring out the colours in furniture or walls, experiment with paint. Start with a range of three differently sized terracotta pots in the same shape, and buy some sample cans of paint. You can have fun with stencils or use tape to mask bands around the pots and paint the rest. Or paint all the pots in one pale or base colour and then add vertical stripes, using two more toning colours. If you take a fine paint brush and draw a line down the centre of each stripe with another of the colours, or the base colour, you end up with an effect rather like wallpaper. Varnish to seal the paint, fill all three with the same plain foliage plant and then group together for effect.

Glazed earthenware or ceramic containers will hold moisture better than plain terracotta, but are

17. Elegant pot.	**18.** Koru planter.	**19.** Stone vessel.

21 Antique dealer Michael Trapp has a collection of magnificent antique urns, carefully placed for maximum effect in his Connecticut garden.

22 The succulent Flapjacks (*Kalanchoe thyrsifolia*) is the perfect choice for a large terracotta urn in a roof top garden by designer Peter Nixon.

23 These huge sculptural urns in the Quillota Garden, Chile, add an air of history and repose to the contemplative atmosphere of a quiet corner.

capable of cracking in very low temperatures, so it pays to check whether they are frost-resistant if you live in an area with cold winters. The positive aspects are colour, pattern and usually competitive prices, unless these receptacles are made individually by artisans rather than mass-produced.

Like terracotta, stoneware is another traditional option and is often particularly handsome and long-lasting. These days, however, concrete has almost overtaken it in popularity as it usually comes in sharp, contemporary forms that lend themselves to clean lines and modern styling. If you prefer traditional stone but can't stretch the budget that far, look at the various colour washes available for concrete. You will be able to replicate that Tuscan or Turkish look relatively easily.

Crushed marble is the other heavyweight alternative. It makes for extremely strong, long-lasting containers, often copied directly from ancient Greek and Roman statuary. Again, it's a matter of personal taste and the look of your home. Hypertufa is a popular, substitute for tufa, a kind of easily pitted volcanic rock, and do-it-yourself types will enjoy the challenge of making their own from a mixture of cement, sand and peat.

Wooden containers, such as used wine barrels, bring to mind the cottage gardens so popular towards the end of last century. Eventually, they tend to rot out at the bottom but by then you will be well and truly ready for a change anyway. The larger ones will take a large shrub or small tree. To prolong the

22. Roof top urn.	**23.** Aged urns.

24 In reference to the architecture of a typical New Zealand bungalow, Trish Bartleet designed these bluestone planters so that they flare out at the bottom.

25 A collection of chimineas at Quillota Garden look ornamental, but when lit add flickering flames and welcome warth to the garden at night.

26 The form of most jugs is inherently pleasing, making them ideal as garden ornaments and, in this case, directing the eye towards the ocean view beyond.

27 The enigmatic simplicity of this Indian clay pot has been brought to the fore through its inspired placement by Eckersley Stafford Design in an area planted with a free flowing groundcover and framed by trees.

lifespan, drill drainage holes in the bottom and line with plastic, or paint the inside with a sealant. Large industrial wooden containers are fabulous where a built-in bed is not practicable. Like raised beds, they are much easier to care for than ground-level plantings as no bending is involved. The plants are also more easily appreciated at that height.

Versailles tubs are the ultimate in elegance – perfect in a traditional setting that calls for a matching pair of containers with the unmistakable stamp of French chic. Once used for citrus trees to supply the château of Louis XIV, the Sun King, they stood outside in the summer and were taken in to the orangerie each winter for protection from the cold. Such tubs are expensive. Some suppliers provide ready-made galvanised liners, complete with pre-drilled holes. These help to keep the plants moist, besides protecting the wood. Both Versailles tubs and wine barrels can be jet-propelled into the twenty-first century by the simple addition of colour. For a smart, ultra-sophisticated look, paint them all black or white and use in pairs or line them up in serious numbers down the length of an outdoor living room.

Window-boxes and containers hanging from walls have always been useful for brightening large, dull, vertical surfaces. Available in terracotta, wire baskets or variations on the wrought iron theme, they need to be firmly attached or even built into the walls themselves to make sure they don't fall. The iron

24. Bluestone planters.

25. Antique chimineas.

26. Tall jug.

27. Indian clay pot.

28 Stylish galvanised steel planters filled with *Yucca elephantipes* add serious impact to a narrow ledge beside a pool.

29 Designed by Rod Barnett, who was inspired from the famous Brazilian landscape architect Roberto Burle Marx, these wall-hung planters owe their mouth-watering colours to Mexican architect Luis Barragán.

30 Placing three bright-blue rectangular planter boxes at different angles and filling them with easy-care plants proved to be a clever and cost-effective way of dealing with a small sloping plot in front of a town house.

must be galvanised and powder-coated to prevent rusting. (That said, old French urns look all the better with a trace of rust.) Wooden window-boxes can be decorated to suit their position. If you live by the sea, gather shells and glue them on or add garlands of threaded ones. Silvery grey succulents reflect the sea and will cope with hot, dry conditions. In a smart urban environment go for sleek foliage or a single cool flower colour for a stylish look.

Plastic and fibreglass copies of most standard pots are easily obtained today and can prove a sensible alternative in places where it is difficult to keep the soil moist, even when wetting agents and water storage granules are added to the potting mix. These lightweight versions also come into their own on roof gardens and balconies where heavy pots are not an option.

Ponga pots, made from the highly textured stems of the silver tree-fern, make excellent containers in a natural, bush-like or shady setting. Old concrete wash-tubs can be pressed into service but they have only one plughole each for drainage, so plant accordingly or your precious seedlings will drown. You can fill the bottom with old crocks – broken bits of pots – and rocks or stones, then add screwed up newspaper to bulk it up before tipping the potting mix in. This will reduce costs and help absorb excess moisture.

28. Galvanised steel.

29. Borrowed planters.

30. Planter boxes.

31. Mosaic pot.

31 Kevin Kilsby demonstrates his mastery of mosaic art with this enormous, winning specimen in his own garden in Mt Albert, Auckland.

32 These glowing stacked pots are typical of the bright colourful containers created by Morris and James, Matakana.

33 A beautiful example of the bold abstract art of the women of the Ndebele tribe of southern Africa, who have for generations embellished their mud houses with these strikingly simple, timeless patterns.

34 Grouping similar or compatible pots dramatically increases their impact, as demonstrated here by the work of Nicholas Brandon and Rosemarie McClay.

32. Colourful stacks.

33. Collector's item.

34. Pot collection.

35 Circular ceramic disks from old telephone poles make an innovative water feature in a container nestled into Vivien Papich's garden.

36 Shells have been used as decoration for centuries, and pots make excellent surfaces. Mr Michie, the original owner of this Kaitaia property, made good use of a ready supply and added paint for a complete transformation.

37 Master potter and sculptor, railway enthusiast and conservationist Barry Brickell created this smoking pot for special effect at Driving Creek Potteries and Railway, near Coromandel.

Finally, if you place your containers as high as possible on pedestals or garden furnishings, you will greatly increase their impact. Fine antique pots and beautifully designed and crafted contemporary ones need perfect placement, not additional plant life, to bring out their best. They make ideal focal points at the end of a walkway or rising from one side to balance an asymmetrical arrangement.

Don't limit your planting to a 'large pot equals large plant' mentality. A tall, symmetrical planter of aluminium, steel or concrete can look amazing with a low topping of plain green such as a dense patch of clipped miniature buxus or the more free-flowing effect of mondo grass. Multiply by all means, but keep both pots and plants within a narrow range: terracotta, for example, with a green and white planting theme, never fails to refresh. Above all, keep it simple.

35. Telephone pot.

36. Shell pots.

37. Smoking pot.

Adding structures to the garden is a powerful way of defining certain areas and making them more user-friendly. From obelisks to pergolas, bridges to boardwalks, they enhance our experience outside.

structures

1. Blue obelisks.

2. Wooden frames.

❶ (Previous page) Three little vegetable beds would be exactly that without these striking blue obelisks – both functional and highly ornamental – bestowing instant 'potager' status.

❷ Freestanding wooden frames give this area of Peter Brady's garden definition, while maintaining the free-flowing effect of the ferns and subtropical planting.

❸ A fine metal pergola provides a strong, yet light touch to a contemporary formal garden in the country.

❹ A beautifully proportioned metal pergola covered in the rose Michèle Meilland in Mrs Rencoret's large garden in Santiago, Chile, designed by Juan Grimm.

Like walls, screens and gates at the boundaries, structures inside a property give the garden a vertical aspect that can radically alter the effect. Think of a planting scheme on the ground and then imagine the same colours and textures set aloft on a pergola or tripod of some kind – instant drama. Shade, protection and privacy are important benefits, especially where taller houses and apartment blocks overlook city gardens. Structures close to the house or even attached to it must take into account the architecture and style of the main dwelling so that they harmonise with or complement it. Further away, within the garden – even if it is a tiny one – you can let your imagination go mad. In fact, coming upon an unexpected feature like a hidden arbour or a cleverly disguised shed will often provide the visitor with that x factor that lifts it out of the ordinary.

Apart from the practical advantages, structures give you the chance to express your own individual personality within your garden in the strongest way of all. A single statement in the form of an archway or a summerhouse immediately announces your personal preferences and sets the tone in a manner that smaller expressions can only hint at. You might already have some elements in place and feel nervous

3. Metal pergola.	**4.** Rose pergola.

5 Landscape designer Ben McMaster has used a connecting half-spiral of metal hoops, or angled arches, covered in hops as a novel way of defining an entrance path.

6 Designer Cilla Cooper creates continuity by installing blue arches that span the changes in level in this garden.

7 Jacqueline Aust created this sculpture made from stainless steel plates at the entrance to the bush on the Brick Bay Sculpture Trail.

8 Rustic-looking manuka logs form a strong, natural archway for the rose Olympic Gold and a kiwifruit vine above a series of steps at The Giant's House in Akaroa.

5. Joined hoops.

6. Blue arches.

7. Decision Arc.

8. Manuka archway.

9 Brigid Maire of Designpoint came up with a sleek modern pergola backed by a large mirror to display the self-watering antipodes planter and native series of pots from Morris and James, Ellerslie Flower Show, 2007.

10 A well-designed traditional pergola is given a smart contemporary look by landscape designer Ben McMaster of Christchurch.

11 The perfectly proportioned simplicity of this little arbour exactly matches the wooden seat and white wisteria covering it.

about stamping your own taste on someone else's work. It's your garden now: go for it. In ten years' time you'll wish you had done just that instead of living in the shadow of your mother-in-law or the previous owners. It doesn't necessarily mean pulling down a structure and replacing it – you may well be able to transform it by the simple means of a coat of paint. Alternatively you could add to it by attaching a trellis-like screen and growing climbers there. Specialist recycling shops have demolition timber, pieces of old fretwork, windows, doors and other decorations that might bring about a completely different look if added to the existing structure. If you want something substantial, like a changing room for the swimming pool, a sleepout or a garage, it will be a job for the professionals. On the other hand, if it's a garden shed or a playhouse for the kids, have some fun and see what you can do with paint, a shelf or two for collections of pots and tools, maybe a mirror, or other found objects. Children will love decorating their own outdoor den and it is a mistake to provide them with a ready-made 'house', leaving nothing whatsoever to the imagination. You will be amazed at their ingenuity if you just leave them to it. By all means let them have any old bricks or boards and household extras such as rags, sheets, rugs or mats

10. Wooden pergola.

11. Simple arbour.

⓬ Plain wooden pergolas are supported and embellished by the Moorish-inspired arched trellis design at this entranceway.

⓭ A minimalist metal pergola and concrete framed 'windows' emphasise and define the sculptural items and plants bordering this courtyard.

⓮ Simplicity is the answer for a pergola belonging to a modern home. Extending from the deck, it frames a group of cacti in pots.

and jars, pots, pans and so on if they ask, but don't take over; you are just providing the set and they won't get any sense of satisfaction if it is not their own work.

Structures fall into two main camps – those that we can spend time in while we are outside and those we look at – they strike the eye because of their height, strong shape or special qualities. We want to feel free from prying eyes in our own backyards, and structures above our heads can give us that intimate feeling. They also balance the tall walls and houses of our own properties and those of our immediate neighbours. What's more, spending time outside is a much more pleasant experience if you have structures to provide some shelter from the elements. A summer-house, for example, will allow you to extend the outdoor season by offering you protection from chilly winds in spring and autumn, besides a fierce sun in summer.

Structures can be used as plant supports or they may be so well designed and built that they can stand unadorned, revealing their craftsmanship in line and detail. Overhead structures include pergolas, arbours, arches, gazebos, pavilions and summer-houses. Tripods and obelisks are strong vertical features used mainly for plant support, while in gardens with sizeable expanses of water, bridges provide special opportunities for artistic expression. Boardwalks too are useful and sometimes essential in sandy, muddy

12. Treillage.   **13.** Architectural design.

14. Desert pergola.

15. Industrial might.

16. Streamlined pergola.

17. Columns.

15 Designed by architect Borja Huidobro and landscape architect Juan Grimm, Papudo on the central coast of Chile features stunning structures such as this sheltered sun spot.

16 The strong blue lines of this pergola define the wooden seating courtyard area by the swimming pool.

17 Traditional columns always add strength to a design, and here they focus the harbour view as well as supporting a roof for outdoor living.

18 An off-white pergola covers a walkway and offsets lush subtropical planting beside a large swimming pool.

or boggy areas. They can turn problem areas into surprisingly attractive landscapes.

Pergolas are open overhead structures that can be covered with climbing plants or left bare. They are either long architectural creations moving people in a certain direction, rather like a covered way, or they are used to cover a space such as a deck, effectively turning it into an outdoor room. The first kind leads somewhere: to a significant view, a building or focal point at the end of a path. The second extends the indoor living space outside, into the world of fresh air and plants. The term 'pergola' is also used to refer to frame-like structures consisting of upright supports, with a single beam linking them at the top. These are often used to encircle a specific area of the garden, such as a large rose garden, or the edge of an area raised above the surrounding landscape. The simplicity and potential strength of a single solid frame should not be underestimated – it can make a huge difference to your garden by adding solidity to a shapeless collection of shrubby plants or by attracting the eye to a particular view or vantage point.

Arbours are usually protected nooks away from the house, providing a light overhead cover for a garden seat so that you can sit and read or daydream in relative peace. They may also have sides but are unlikely to provide much protection. Traditionally, they would have been made of trellis, light timber or

18. Modern pergola.

19 A beautifully designed and built wooden obelisk is a feature at Stonecrop Gardens, Cold Spring, New York, originally the home of Anne and Frank Cabot.

20 Festooned with lilac wisteria, a blue pergola gives outdoor diners a chance to enjoy the sight and scent of spring.

21 Designed by Anthony Paul, a blue trellis structure provides a sheltered spot from which to view the garden.

22 A blue trellis around a natural timber pergola frame screens the neighbouring property from a beachside garden.

fine ironwork, but you could be innovative and use a stainless-steel frame, bamboo or a combination of curved tent supports as the basis or your own modern-day interpretation of the form. A combination of trellis and plywood can be stained or painted and shaped to imitate a traditional style for a fraction of the cost of a ready-made or professionally built arbour.

Arches define an area and are generally built strongly to support climbing plants. They may be used to cover a gate, as in a lych gate, at the entrance to a garden or property, or they may indicate the boundary point between different garden rooms. Placed side by side, a series of simple curved arches form a colonnade or even a cloister of sorts, and if you put a number of them behind each other, you have an archway. The intricate construction and carpentry required for a lych gate, taken from traditional styles once used at the entrance to churchyards where the coffin lay before burial, is commonly left bare.

Gazebos are open-sided square, oblong or hexagonal structures with pitched roofs. They may be positioned at a high point in the terrain to take in a view over the countryside or perhaps look downwards over a flight of stairs to a major feature such as a pond or lake. The sides can be filled in up to a certain point, often above bench seating around the inside, but not high enough to obscure the view.

Pavilions and summer-houses are sometimes so soundly constructed they can literally be used as

19. Wooden obelisk.

20. Wisteria display.

21. Blue gazebo.

22. Beach retreat.

23. Greek Folly.

23 Designed by architect John D'Anvers, a Greek folly with a pebble star mosaic on the ground makes this space in a garden by Trish Waugh a strong destination point.

24 Located at Old Westbury Gardens, New York, this pavilion is typical of the elegantly detailed architecture of houses and gardens from the early twentieth century.

25 A fine example of a traditional brick and glass, European-style conservatory at Quinta Nicolasa in Santiago, Chile.

24. Victorian pavilion.

25. Conservatory.

outdoor rooms, where furnishings will stay dry whatever the weather. This makes them perfect as retreats, where you can work or rest away from the comings and goings of the main household. Both children and adults will enjoy sharing drinks and meals in the relative seclusion they provide, outside in pleasant natural surroundings. Contemporary designs have moved far from the original classical versions and may suit both modern and some older styles of architecture.

Glass and the modern alternatives available today can be incorporated into an overhead pergola to provide extra shelter from rain, or even added on to the side or end of a garden shed to make a small glasshouse for tender plants. Brush already tied together is cheap and useful to layer on to a wall that is not attractive, or it can be framed to make a screen to hide utilitarian objects. Corrugated iron should not be overlooked either as a practical base for structures: it can look amazing painted a rusty red or dark green, nearly black. The finer kind now available again can look good left naturally silver.

Tripods and obelisks are a familiar sight in large potagers or vegetable gardens, where they have been used for centuries to support a vast range of edible plants. They work equally well for many ornamentals and their tall triangular or cone shape presents a marvellous opportunity for introducing the excitement of vivid colour, or the more natural appeal of cane and willow, into the garden. Being relatively inexpensive, they are one of the simplest and most affordable ways to introduce an element of height

26. Lakeside summer-house.

26 A soundly constructed summer-house jutting out over a lake is the ideal way to view the water, especially when it is covered in the rose Cathayensis in full bloom.

27 Clark Abbott built the dry stone walls and charmingly rustic summer-house at Greagh Gardens, near Whangarei.

28 Crafted out of fine logs, this rustic summer-house in a garden on Long Island, New York, fits well in its woodland setting.

and drama. A pyramid shape can be made of wood, iron or steel for a more solid support but don't forget that metal can get hot in the sun and the plants will not enjoy that.

Bridges are another category of structure that has changed radically in the last decade or so. Once limited to the bright red bridges inspired by the orient and plain, solid wood affairs (entirely serviceable but perhaps a little unimaginative), they can now occasionally be remarkable works of art, in both private and public spaces. The reaction is invariably positive as people appreciate the beauty and enjoy the clever effects some of these edifices offer. Like every other structure in the garden, they provide an opportunity for design that is not just functional but also offers superior form and sometimes even wit.

If you intend to cover your outdoor structures with plants, they need to be strongly built as they will give way with alarming speed if they are not up to the task: plants can quickly become massively heavy to support. Wood and iron or steel are the most common materials, although bamboo and willow have their place for lighter tripods and screen-like rod effects.

Structures that will be covered with plants need careful thought as they may be bare for several months in the winter. You won't want to be looking at a naked, ugly support for that long, so you have a

27. Country summer-house.

28. Woodland summer-house.

29 A red bridge arches across the pond at Clive and Nicki Higgie's Paloma Gardens, Fordell, Wanganui.

30 Worthy of the Romans, this solid stone bridge will last for generations, providing a picturesque focal point and access to the rest of the garden.

31 Named after the jointed rush – a native plant found in coastal marshland and estuaries – Oioi Bridge by Virginia King at Connells Bay Sculpture Park, Waiheke, shows what is possible when a sculptor turns their hand to designing an object usually conceived from a purely practical point of view.

choice – either cover it with an evergreen climber or design and build a structure that will be pleasing even when it is fully revealed. Garden centres have a wide range of tripods and ornamental supports in green- or black-coated metal that will fulfil your basic needs, and they are not necessarily expensive.

Do your research and choose your plants with care so that they will give you the effect you want: beautiful flowers, stunning foliage, perfume – or a combination of all three. If you want to grow wisteria, for example, you will need to trim and train it to give the best possible display of scented lilac, pink or white blossom in early spring and impressive structure when it sheds its flowers and leaves. Some roses have blooms that stand straight up from the branch – hopeless if you want to see them from below. Substitute varieties with weaker necks that allow the flowers to flop down into view. Sweet peas will romp up a wigwam or tripod of bamboo canes, and jasmines are the obvious answer for a bower of perfume, especially in the evening. Some are particularly rampant, though, and will quickly become thugs, so check before you plant.

29. Red bridge.	**30.** Stone bridge.

31. Sculptural bridge.

32. Blue decking.

32 Water features strongly in gardens designed by Anthony Paul, resulting in superb creations like this blue deck stretching over a water lily pond.

33 Boardwalks can be the most practical and attractive way of moving people from one area to another, especially when water is present.

34 Crossing the sand dunes to reach the beach would be difficult and damaging without the existence of a wooden boardwalk at Castlecliff, Wanganui.

A little planning, a little flair – and everyday activities like eating and drinking become another experience altogether when they take place out of doors under a canopy of green. Place your outdoor table beneath a pergola draped with Boston ivy, which will keep out the overhead heat in summer, then look superb in fiery autumn colours, before dying away to let the winter sun and light through again. Or substitute grapes if you want fruit for that table.

It is easy to make your garden look inviting with a little ingenuity, and without the huge outlay many permanent structures demand. Colour is the obvious solution but think in terms of fabrics or combine them with paint. On the flimsiest of frames, with a few wires attached, you can drape flowing fabric to create an arbour of your own. A sun umbrella or awning will be a lot more affordable than a built structure and it is instant, whereas trees can take years to grow to a size where they provide adequate shade. In a trice, cushions can suggest the silky opulence of the east, or the desert oases of Arabia. A striped rug or woven flax mat on the ground, a cheerful tablecloth and some retro china from a second-hand shop will turn a basic outdoor space into a haven. Add some scented candles, lanterns, and a brazier to create an inviting atmosphere at night.

33. Boardwalk. **34.** Beach access.

Why yearn for that prohibitively expensive piece of sculpture when you could create your own masterpiece out of 'found' objects? It's a matter of looking at the potential around you.

rustic

1. Faithful servant.

❶ (Previous page) Allowed to retire peacefully in the shed, an old red truck is not only decorative – its tray is used for storing firewood.

❷ Attached to a rail fence, old branches from felled trees create an interesting pattern and blend naturally with the planting.

❸ Vegetable gardens have an earthy reality that lends itself to this unpainted version of the picket fence.

❹ Designer Liz Mackmurdie created this woven willow fence with tea tree stakes to contain a vegetable garden.

Gardens present us with the opportunity to toss caution to the winds. Once outside, we find the rules disappear and we can indulge a sense of fantasy and personal expression with a freedom that far exceeds our comfort zone as interior decorators. If you are convinced that you are creatively challenged, try breaking the mould with small collections. Everyday objects take on a whole new image when they are brought together. Grasses, seed heads, pods or pine cones gathered in a basket, upturned terracotta pots in a group, shells in a glass jar – you can do it. The hard part is taking that first tiny step.

In its widest sense, the term rustic goes beyond the obvious one of anything plain and sturdy, related or appropriate to the country. It can also be used to express the idea of folk culture, or anything simple and unsophisticated. In gardening terms, this means creating your own vision of an outdoor space filled with whatever takes your fancy: old tools, bottles and glass objects, weathered wood of any description from driftwood to manuka, brushwood and willow branches, old gates, railway sleepers, bridge timber, fence battens, swamp kauri and tree stumps. On top of that you can indulge a passion for recycling, second to none.

2. Rustic fence.	**3.** Earthy reality.

5. Found objects.

5 Other people's unwanted old treasures find a new home on a wacky wall by Ian Douglas of Waiheke Island.

6 Sculptor Jeff Thomson has a veritable flock of corrugated iron hens and roosters outside his studio in Helensville, north of Auckland.

7 Gum tree logs cushioned with thyme make a comfortable seat at Christine and Tony Peek's garden, Woodbridge.

8 Dan Rutherford created this log wall, complete with a window, at his home in Cashmere Hills, Christchurch.

6. Chooks.

7. Log seat.

8. Log wall.

9 Nothing ages wood like lichen growing on it. A wooden gate and venerable posts look the part at Richard Mathews' and Seng Cheah's garden at Waimauku.

10 A patterned brick wall and intricately cut out, rusty-looking metal gate welcomes visitors to Driving Creek Potteries and Railway on the Coromandel Peninsula.

11 Using milled timber and driftwood from the beach at Castlecliff, Wanganui, sculptor Rick Rudd has developed palisade terraces on the hillside below his home.

9. Lichen-covered gate.　　**10.** Rusty gate.

Another approach is to take whatever nature provides and use your creativity to turn that into a work of art. Wherever you live, there will be a ready supply of raw material to fuel the flames of your particular obsession. It might be plants or animals, man-made paraphernalia, the beach or wild coast, the farm or natural bush, mountains, rivers, lakes, other people's junk, bikes, planes, cars, boats, bits of old buildings including corrugated iron, staircases, church pews, mirrors – whatever. What you need to unlock the door to a whole new private paradise is found simply by looking at the world around you with fresh eyes.

While we embrace the new and well-designed with eager arms, it is not until the old and once useful has become rare that we are suddenly seized with nostalgia. We look back on its attributes with a warm feeling of times past and feel comforted if we can still enjoy it somewhere in our lives – not as a working article, but in a new role as a stage prop for plants or for pure decoration and garden ornament.

Let us begin with life on the farm. Just a hundred years ago this was a totally different experience than it is today. Think of all the tools and machinery, now residing in museums or rotting in fields, that could have found a place in a country garden. Some, such as the wagon wheel, have almost become clichés but it is clever placement and innovative use – trying something new and fresh – that will lift such finds above the trite and hackneyed. Old gardening tools make fantastic decoration: on walls where nothing will grow, leaning together in a tripod arrangement or crossed over each other to fill in a gate or make the backdrop to a garden seat. Think small and recycle the excess contents of the tool box by setting flat

11. Palisade terraces.

12. Plant nursery.

13. Sculpture.

14. Pumice columns.

12 Beach timber and driftwood are ideal materials
to make an arch over the propagation nursery at
Rick Rudd's coastal property.

13 It takes skill and breadth of vision to see
the sculptural possibilities in objects, including
pumice and timber found on the beach.

14 Pumice has long been a popular medium for
sculpture as it is easy to carve and thread, as
illustrated by these columns of Trish Bartleet's at
the entrance to a house.

15 Coastal and alpine plants clothe a steep bank,
terraced with driftwood at Rick Rudd's.

items like spanners into a square of cement as a paving arrangement or just hanging them on the wall. Old horseshoes and iron drain covers can be reincarnated in either of these ways as well.

The farm dairy of days past is a rich source of treasures ranging from milking stools, buckets and cans to the stainless-steel bowls used to separate the cream from the milk, large flat skimmers, and butter churns or pats. Use your imagination and convert some of these into plant containers or a collage of themed decorative items.

Anything to do with horses is ripe for the picking. Old harnesses, the horseshoes already mentioned, tools for the blacksmith's forge, bits and stirrups, grooming gear, feeding buckets and troughs can all be pressed into service again as collections on display or as water features and plant holders.

Rural properties with long histories can usually be relied upon to supply old building material and aged fencing posts and battens. Look to the shearing shed for more inspiration – old hand shears and early cutters and machine parts, presses and wool sorting tables – anything might be capable of metamorphosis. In the days when farmers cut their own firewood by hand, crosscut saws and axes were essential items. Circular saw blades and tools such as scythes, sickles and reapers from that era can be used to create your own mixed-media sculptures or simply displayed together. Sieves used to separate

15. Driftwood
terraces.

16 Piled driftwood becomes beachside sculpture and found timber makes a fence at Rick Rudd's Castlecliff garden.

17 A simple criss-cross pattern of rustic branches from fallen trees sets off a sprawling oak-leaved hydrangea, Snow Queen (*Hydrangea quercifolia*), to perfection in a garden designed by Nancy McCabe, Connecticut.

18 A view down the iron garden through to the sea, overlooking the 'rubble rockery' at Rick Rudd's inspired garden of recycled objects.

16. Beach path.	**17.** Rustic fence.

oats from chaff make wonderful plant containers: why not group them on an old table or shelf and match the plants for impact? Alternatively you could tier them on supports arranged down a wall and grow trailing plants in them. Ropes and chains that have seen better days make simple barriers at the corners of boundaries, or pointers to direct people through the garden and keep them off a special bed.

The garden shed presents a perfect opportunity for displays of garden-related objects. You can't go wrong with terracotta pots as they are fundamentally good-looking. Stack them upside down randomly to brighten a dull corner outside or get seriously artistic with an arrangement on a bench or shelf. The same goes for trugs and wicker baskets used for gathering flowers for the house. A traditional filling of pine cones, grasses, rushes or bunches of dried flowers will complete the picture.

Old teapots, jugs and watering cans can all be pressed into service again just by placing them in attractive groups. Fill them with plants or paint them in a variety of cheerful colours for a sun-soaked Mediterranean effect.

Brightly striped canvas will bring an old deck-chair or folding director's chair back to life. If old ones are not to be found, buy them new as cheaply as possible and age them by sanding down the wood, rubbing the surface with a wax candle and then painting – white for a white-washed look or one of those aqua shades that bring the French countryside to mind. Use something like a kitchen steel pad or wire wool to rub off the paint, revealing some of the wood, and let nature do the rest. Large covered cushions will complement the deck chairs and make plain old wooden and wicker benches and sofas far more

18. Iron garden.

19. Orange lichen.

20. Tree rings.

21. Rusty rejects.

22. Ground cover.

23. Circles upon circles.

24. Farm objects.

25. Red pebbles.

26. Beach plants.

19 Concrete pillars blend into the landscape as they slowly become covered in orange lichen.

20 Collections of glass and ceramics from the beach displayed in tree rings.

21 Rusty old rejects find a new home in the iron garden part of Rick Rudd's hillside beach garden.

22 *Raoulia hookeri* grows through a collection of shells from the beach.

23 The circular motif is repeated as planters, pavers and vessels for various collections.

24 Old agricultural items become sculptural shapes beckoning at the sea.

25 By isolating a collection of objects within a ring, Rick Rudd draws our attention to the singular beauty of the items within it.

26 Groundcover plants and native coastal varieties make the garden their home.

27 Astelia terraces and shell beds blend into a carpeting blanket of *Raoulia hookeri*.

comfortable and inviting to lounge about in outdoors. Take yourself on a trip down memory lane to the seaside or lakeside bach for a moment. Enamel cooking ware, colanders and wash basins; coal or wood ranges; water tanks; deck-chairs; collections of shells, stones, driftwood, buoys, boats, oars, lifebelts, anchors, fishing nets and old rods – the list is endless. What about filling old crayfish pots with stones to look like gabions or using them to support plants that would normally need staking? Sea eggs or kina make novel sculptures when attached to the top of thick wire or metal rods and grouped together. The beach and coastline have spawned some of the most eccentric and unique gardens in the world. If you are lucky enough to live in such a stimulating environment, your own version is closer than a dream– it's on your doorstep.

If home is in a town or city, foraging is the way to go. Council-organised inorganic rubbish collections, where everyone puts out their unwanted household articles, will turn up some extraordinary finds. What is of no further use to one person can be gold to another who is looking for objects with a different potential purpose in mind. Old chests of drawers can be converted into containers and the open drawers filled with a range of trailing and hanging plants. Shop models and dressmakers' dummies can become the cheapest of sculptural finds, and clever gardeners will be able to use them in ways that question or

27. Pool coutryard.

28 Old wagon wheels propped against tree trunks in the Chiñihue Garden, Melpilla, Chile, make a nostalgic reference to the past.

29 Solid wooden wheels set in the ground make an interesting collection of sculptural forms in the same garden.

30 Sculptor Rick Rudd has amassed abandoned objects to create an iron garden at the bottom of the hillside on his property at Castlecliff.

mock or simply poke fun at the human condition. Treadle sewing machines, trestle tables, old tea wagons and butlers' trays all make excellent pot plant stands or surfaces for displaying collections. If the iron treadle is all that remains of the sewing machine, it could join a collection of other old household items hanging on an outside wall.

Old coppers from the days before washing machines are often to be seen polished up and pressed into service as firewood receptacles, umbrella stands, plant containers and purely decorative ornaments outside where they soon gain that fine blue-green tinge or patina that is so attractive. Bedsteads and the coils that supported mattresses before they were innersprung can become, respectively, backdrops to outdoor seats and quirky spiralling supports in a large container. Old boots, painted and filled with undemanding plants like succulents and cacti, look amazing grouped en masse. Broken ladders can be attached to a wall and used to support climbing plants. If you have several, arrange them in a triangle as a fresh take on the tripod – or as a pyramid.

Old chimney pots make excellent sculptural pieces. Just stand them on a stone plinth or make one out of concrete, then plaster and colour-wash it to make it look older and more in keeping with its load.

Modes of transport beyond the horse-drawn cart and gig throw up plenty of possibilities for garden

28. Wagon wheels.	**29.** Wooden wheels.

30. Iron gate.

31. Whimsical pond.

32. Roman clock.

33. Crazy garden.

31 At his home in southern England, Ivan Hicks gives full vent to his childlike fascination with the possibilities of odd and unusual found objects in the creation of a typically surreal, 'off-the-wall' garden.

32 A giant clock is just one of a multitude of strange machines at the Waiau Waterworks, an interactive garden on the 309 Road that runs across the Coromandel Peninsula.

33 The End of the Century shop and backyard garden in Onehunga epitomises the possibilities of combining plants with everyday objects.

34 Ivan Hicks has filled his own garden with whimsical, nostalgic objects such as this large shapely window frame, which is slowly becoming overgrown by plants.

35 Humour is an underlying element throughout the Waiau Waterworks, as shown in this witty sculpture of a cyclist in the middle of a pond.

ornament. Old wheelbarrows are perfect for collections of pots and for growing alpine plants or tiny specimens that would get lost in a large bed or border. You could paint your barrow in a contrasting colour to set off a collection of spring bulbs, for example, and wheel it away to rest when they are past their best, or change the pots to a freshly flowering batch. Used tyres have had bad press for their kitsch appearance in the past but they are useful for protecting young plants in harsh, windswept environments such as an exposed coastline. Think outside the square and pass on the white paint. Abandoned cars, tractors and trucks are usually eyesores but they don't have to be. Half covered in an attractive climbing plant or by a dilapidated old shed, they can be quite appealing as nature slowly reclaims its ground.

Old concrete posts or vertical slabs can be randomly set out in a disjointed circle of standing stones in homage to Stonehenge and other ancient sculptural landmarks. Alternatively, they can be laid out like the spokes of a wheel around an old circular trough buried in the ground to make a water feature or a container for a spectacular plant. The areas in between the 'spokes' can be filled with gravel or, if the trough is filled with water, low-growing plants such as herbs.

Posts or poles can add intrigue to a garden in many ways. They can be painted a plain colour or differing colours, for example in swirling, ribbon-like markings reminiscent of a maypole or a barber's

34. Arched window frame.

35. Bicycle.

36. Tree trunk.

37. Knotted seat.

38. Crafted seat.

39. Telephone poles.

40. Armchair.

36 A sawn tree trunk makes a perfectly rustic seat to rest on beneath a tree.

37 The shape of a piece of weathered timber lent itself to this home-made garden seat.

38 A favourite place to sit and enjoy a view over the garden in the 'garrigue' or dry area on a Woodbridge hillside.

39 Recycled telephone poles add a bit of novelty and history to a garden seat.

40 These slightly bizarre-looking arms, made from branches, are nevertheless a practical addition to this garden chair.

41 Beloved of gardeners everywhere, manuka (or tea tree) lends itself to a thousand uses in the garden, where it always looks at home.

shop. You might place them close together in a row to block off an area or in a more open, relaxed way as a purely visual barrier.

Tin cans nailed onto a wooden stick figure and strung upside down, so they clang together, make an effective scarecrow, gradually mellowing as they succumb to rust. Terracotta pots can be used for the same purpose and in both cases the top container can be filled with a suitable plant to give the scarecrow flowing locks. Chicken wire can be stretched over a frame to make a plant support or topiary figure. Sometimes it is easier to bend it around a filling of any bulked material to create the figure of a bird or animal. Used without a solid base, it becomes a ghostly, ethereal outline of human or animal forms.

Instead of mosaic, cover a tall pillar or any suitable object with recycled patterned tiles to create a kind of Portuguese or Spanish effect. Alternatively, use brightly coloured plain tiles in contrasting patterns. Pebble mosaics are another form of decoration that anyone can try in a simple form, although it pays to attend a course or follow a manual to find out how to get the best results. Finding pebbles that are similar and others that contrast in colour and size may prove to be the hardest part. Basically it involves pressing your pebbles vertically into dry-mix cement in a pleasing pattern, then finishing with another layer of sand and cement brushed into the cracks. The pebbles need to be tightly packed to provide an even

41. Manuka seat.

42 Decorated with a snake of fine mosaic, a solid railway sleeper perched on bricks makes a useful bench seat in Kevin Kilsby's colourful garden.

43 Jeff Thomson can turn corrugated iron into anything – even a comfortable chair. This one is in Becroft Garden on the shores of Lake Pupuke, Takapuna.

44 Beautifully crafted from gnarled old branches, these unusual chairs add an earthy touch to the terrace at Whitley, a heritage house and garden in the Southern Highlands, New South Wales.

surface, otherwise they might prove a hazard on which people trip. Local stone or rock can be piled up in simple mounds for a basic sculptural effect as a centrepiece or focal point. Try balancing smooth, flat stones or rocks: begin with larger ones on the bottom and then gradually decrease the size as you work upwards, cementing them in place if necessary as you go. Or place a substantial block or a tall post at the base like a pedestal and secure a few rocks on top. Another approach is to raise a flat slab or wooden board on a few rocks and then repeat the pattern with a few more rocks at each end and with another flat slab on top. Make the top layer finish at a sharp angle so that no one will think to sit or stand on the arrangement, as it won't be entirely stable. You might find you like your stonework so much you wouldn't want to change it for anything else, even if you could.

The same can be done with wood in the form of branches or driftwood. Pumice is easy to work with: being porous and soft, it can easily be fixed to sharp pieces of metal or pointed wood. It makes an ideal sculptural material as you can whittle away with a pocket knife. Children will love creating fierce faces or small animals out of it. Wire can be passed through pumice, too, making it extremely versatile for making a myriad decorative features.

If you haven't got a ready supply of atmospheric, lichen-covered old logs or some bleached driftwood, you can improvise. A log sawn into pennies or circular slabs will give you a supply of magic circles to cover an old garden shed – simply nail them on to the outside, for a log cabin effect.

Children will love a tree house, even if it is a simple platform with a safety barrier round the edge.

42. Railway sleeper.	**43.** Corrugated iron.

44. Gnarled comfort.

45. Elephants

45 One of Jeff Thomson's iconic corrugated iron elephants roams at large in a private garden.

46 There is something endearing about a baby elephant following on after his mother, as this one does.

47 A scarecrow made of terracotta pots reigns supreme at Rathmoy, a country garden near Hunterville.

48 Slumped in an armchair, this snoozing scarecrow is probably not very good at his job.

Climbing up a ladder is a popular challenge and if it is short and light they can pull it up after them. A rope ladder is more difficult to negotiate but can be hauled up more easily. A strong, stout rope with a large knot tied in it a metre or so from the ground will make an ideal swing if there is a tree to hang it from and room to manoeuvre. The best fun is to be had by climbing up on a frame of some kind and then launching into the air on the swing rope. This is only suitable for older children and a soft landing will be required. A basic pulley system or miniature flying fox from a tree house to another fixed point such as an upstairs balcony on the main house will keep children occupied for hours sending treasures and messages back and forth.

After dark, soft ambient lighting will take you and your visitors out. Fixed garden lights are expensive to install and, for the ideal result, need to go in when the garden is first laid out. But you can create that romantic mood in other ways by stringing tiny white fairy lights like the ones used at Christmas time around your outdoor living area. Nothing has quite the same effect as candlelight but the fire danger is real, so work around it. A large, wide glass container with floating candles well below the rim can be pure magic. Fill the bottom with your shell collection for extra effect and use fragrant aromatherapy candles or citronella for insect control. In a sheltered spot, you could grow small-leafed ivy over a rusty old iron candelabra set in a suitable container, producing a grander atmospheric centrepiece.

46. Baby elephant.	**47.** Terracotta scarecrow.	**48.** Sleeping scarecrow.

Creating a sense of illusion in your garden is all about having fun. You can keep your visitors amused and entertained by indulging in a little magical wit and wisdom.

2. Mirror, mirror.

❶ (Previous page) Sculptor Allan Coleman uses chicken wire to create evocative forms such as this illusory tableau of dancers from Sculpture OnShore, 2006.

❷ Mirrors can create stunning effects out of doors, effectively doubling the impact of a garden – to say nothing of the view – as seen here on the terrace of a Parnell townhouse designed by Cilla Cooper.

❸ A small backyard full of native plants is twice the size, courtesy of the mirrors on the wall in a Remuera garden.

❹ A flowering datura and other flamboyant subtropical plants are captured and replayed by means of a large framed mirror in Graeme Ross's Beach Haven garden.

Compare a garden for a moment with a novel, or a play. What will intrigue and enchant the reader, the audience? What keeps them turning the pages and glued to their seats?

Above all else, it is the suspense, the setting of a certain tone, the dropping of hints and clues, the unravelling of a puzzle or mystery, complete with misleading side-steps and dead ends. We want to see what happens when all the skeletons in the cupboard are laid bare, truth is finally revealed and the dilemmas, tensions and misunderstandings are eventually resolved.

With a garden, as with a story in a book or a drama played out on stage, the show is over if all is revealed at the outset, in one quick glance. What will absorb visitors, enticing them to explore further, to follow that path, see what is around the corner, is the sense that all is not as it seems and that there may be something more – hidden, secret, mysterious – a sense of illusion.

Gardeners have indulged this desire for an element of surprise throughout the history of gardening. Sophisticated water tricks were the height of fashion in Renaissance gardens, where they were used to show off the engineering skills that demonstrated man's power over nature. The unsuspecting garden wanderer would unwittingly trigger a spray or jet of water and emerge soaking wet, only to be caught

3. Native reflection.	**4.** Framed mirror.

5 Inspired by Lewis Carroll's book, red and white floral compositions represent giant chess pieces that can be moved around a chequerboard garden, resulting in a mirrored landscape in constant motion.

6 A garden representing life, with the threads we follow constantly crossing over each other and creating endless different possibilities.

7 A series of three free-standing mirrors reflect and multiply different garden views in Dennis Greville's Christchurch garden.

unawares by another practical joke lurking around the corner. Performing statues, complicated maze, secret grottoes, false perspectives and hidden escape routes are all part of our gardening heritage.

These days, the emphasis is more on making the best use of smaller spaces, and the idea of playing with our sense of illusion is an excellent place to start.

The French expression 'trompe-l'oeil' has long been used in gardening terms to cover anything that deceives the eye by means of false perspective or painted scenes and images. By making parallel lines converge we gain the appearance of distance, and the same principle applies to objects becoming smaller and hazier the further away from us they are. It can be enormous fun to try and apply these basic rules of perspective in the garden, especially as gardens become more and more confined. By narrowing paths as they extend away from the viewer, we make them appear longer than they are in reality. You can do the same thing with lines of pots and even plants by placing larger ones in the foreground and then reducing the size the further away they are from the main viewpoint. Why not throw in colour too?

5. Through the Looking Glass.

6. A Word Maze.

7. Reflected seat.

8. Mirrored obelisk.

8 Designer Sayburn Miller inserted a mirrored obelisk into this shady corner of a Stanley Point, Devonport garden to reflect the green and white effects of the surrounding landscape.

9 Artist Jane Watt produced this site-specific work, a temporary camera obscura, for the Westonbirt Arboretum Festival in Gloucestershire, 2004.

10 Water spills smoothly in mesmerising fashion over glass steps in this water feature designed by Trish Bartleet.

Make your plants, pots or structures gradually paler towards the far end of the garden, keeping the stronger hues close to the house.

Glass is magical in the garden and one of the best ways to use it is by installing a mirror or two. Flat mirrors can make a space and all the objects within it appear twice their real size and number, besides making the whole area seem lighter and brighter. Used on different shapes, such as obelisks, screens or spheres, the effect is multiplied, as more of the surroundings will be reflected.

Thoughtful placement is required, so it pays to experiment. Angled effects often work well, especially in corners, and make sure you cover the edges with plants so that the mirrors blend in and the results look natural. Few people will enjoy seeing themselves reflected as they walk up your path, so make sure the mirrors are throwing back desirable objects and views, rather than the viewer. This applies to any glass: large windows in the house, like bi-fold doors for instance, can reflect what is happening in an outdoor living area to strategically placed neighbours, even though the deck, courtyard or pool itself may be out of sight. It also pays to avoid delivering a dazzling blast of reflected sun that will blind your visitors.

Polished metals such as copper and stainless steel have smooth reflective surfaces that can be used to produce a mirror effect – possibly in conjunction with water. Mirrors are usually used for water in the

9. Reflectagon.

10. Glass water feature.

An outdoor dining area in a tiny courtyard is given an exotic twist by the addition of a painted allée appearing to stretch into the distance.

 Designed by Lesley Kennedy for the Westonbirt Arboretum Festival, Gloustershire, this garden containing five metal cubicles, covered on the inside with idyllic landscapes, expressed her concern for environmental problems arising from inorganic waste.

 Gregor Kregar's stainless steel sculpture not only reflects its natural surroundings, it replicates the geometric form of their basic molecular structure.

shoe-box gardens made by children but in the real world a silvery piece of stainless steel would be a safer reflective choice for a small garden, if water itself is not an option. This is definitely the way to go if your garden doubles as a backyard cricket pitch; broken glass is not a possibility you want to have to think about.

Apart from its use in mirrors, glass can be rewarding in other ways in the garden. It has inherently pleasing qualities, being both smooth and clear, or alternatively, coloured and glowing, making it a material that works superbly well with water or in conjunction with a contrasting material like concrete. Coloured medallions or beads of glass make an unusual groundcover or mulch, or you could try them at the base of a water feature.

Light can produce magical illusionary images in a garden. Apart from being practical for lighting paths and alerting you to visitors, you can use it to enhance the sculptural qualities of trees and of course sculptural objects themselves. It works especially well in water, bathing the surroundings in a soft, suffusing gleam. It can be used to draw attention to decorative items such as glass sculptures, water

11. Tented illusion.	**12.** Some things will not grow.

14. Painted view.

14 If you want a harbour view from your swimming pool it is easily done, as shown by Melbourne designers Out From the Blue.

15 By dividing this painted mural by Melissa Langford into five panels and setting it on a wall covered in dense growth, the work itself has been enriched, while at the same time it greatly enhances the courtyard living area by Eckersley Stafford Design, Melbourne.

16 Sydney garden designer Anne Thomson was responsible for this mural, adding interest to the wall of a swimming pool.

features or plants above a pool. Lighting experts use a range of coloured filters to produce amazing effects, no less dramatic than a night at the theatre.

Vistas painted on walls add a sense of mystery as it becomes difficult to distinguish between the real and the imaginary. This works best when it is used within firm outlines or boundaries, such as an arched frame. By adding a false door or an archway at the end of a pathway, you make it look as if there is another space beyond to move into, instead of a dead end. A three-dimensional view painted on a wall to look like a window can enrich a dull shed, for example, making it look inviting and full of fascinating objects. If you want a harbour or sea view, an enticing secret garden, a magnificent Grecian urn, paint one or get someone with sufficient artistic flair to do it for you. The trick is in the surroundings: all the built structures and plants must frame the image to make it look more natural, as if it is part of the actual garden.

15. Painted mural.	**16.** Decorated wall.

17 Terry Stringer is a master of illusion. The viewer who circles this sculpture will be rewarded as a series of hidden images is revealed: a boy's head, a hand raised in blessing, and the drape of cloth that defines the traditional memorial urn.

18 Neil Dawson's stainless steel ball, *Flora*, appears to float above the garden at Ohinetahi, Sir Miles Warren's garden at Governor's Bay.

19 In this mask of Fate by Terry Stringer, the Roman Goddess of Fortune, who carries a goblet to reward and a bridle to restrain, is standing on the head of the artist, instead of the usual globe of the world. The feet and head are brought together in a work whose silhouette makes the outline of a colossal profile, in which the goblet is the eye. The piece is displayed in front of the house designed by Pip Cheshire at Zealandia, itself a sculptural work of art.

Paint is capable of converting the plain and ordinary into the dazzling and unique. It can make you feel as if you are in another part of the world – a searingly hot desert landscape or the balmy tropics, Mexico or Morocco, the Mediterranean or South America, Africa or Fiji. Once you have an image in your head, capture the colours, the essence and the mood with paint and fabric. Your garden should be a source of delight, of fun and sheer escapism, not a serious attempt to prove your horticultural skills to the neighbours. They will be far more appreciative of your attempts to amuse and enchant them with your fresh, innovative approach. Turn disasters into positive events. If a pivotal tree dies, paint it or hang colourful collections of old glass bottles in it. If a favourite pet shuffles off this mortal coil, install a memorial such as a topiary animal, or a sculpture, as a permanent reminder.

The ancient technique of mosaic can completely transform everyday objects into works of art. In the hands of an expert, the effect can be mesmerising, as we are treated to familiar objects covered in swirls of brilliant or subtle colour and pattern, reinvented in original designs courtesy of tile fragments or pieces of china we remember from Grandmother's day. From the letter box at the gate to every conceivable piece of outdoor furnishing, including iron sofas, tables, containers, bare walls and of course

17. Face, Fingers, Fabric. | **18.** Flora.

19. Fortuna.

20. Wooden porthole.

20 A stone outcrop is highlighted through a circular window at Cold Spring, New York.

21 A circular hole in the brick wall at Winterhome, Richard and Susan MacFarlane's garden in Marlborough, extends the view of a long formal pool into a vista.

22 The Chinese Garden at Darling Harbour in Sydney features a traditional circular moongate in an intimate courtyard, offering glimpses of the nearby lake and waterfall.

23 In this Japanese-style garden, Richard Greenwood has used circular windows to echo the round shapes of the boulders and planting in the garden and to enhance the atmosphere of tranquility.

paths, steps and terraces: they can all take on a new and vivid life of their own with a bit of mosaic magic.

Taken to extremes, entire gardens can be filled with mythical settings bursting with strange creatures and imaginary figures until the whole takes on an air of total fantasy. You begin to feel like Alice in Wonderland, a visitor to a dream-like world peopled by apparitions, albeit reassuringly hard, solid, static ones.

Anyone can indulge their creative instincts by experimenting with mosaic. Once you have decided on the pattern you want to use — perhaps by copying a basic design — scale it to fit the required area and mark it out. Cut tiles result in a better, more even effect than broken ones and the way you combine the colours and tones is all important. For home projects, the easiest approach is to use the direct method, where you press the tiles into a small area of cement, or coat each one with cement and then stick it on, leaving gaps for the grout in between just like a professional tiler does. The following day, when it has set completely, you can add the grout, filling all the spaces and wiping off any extra bits with a damp cloth. Leave for 24 hours to dry again before giving it a final polish.

It is also possible to work directly on to fibreglass mesh and then cement the blocks in place. That way you don't have to work outside on site. The same applies to the indirect method, which also gives you a

| **21.** Long view. | **22.** Moongate. | **23.** Peace Garden. |

24. Copper glow.

25. Earth, Fire and Water.

26. Polyhedron construction 1.

24 Designer and artist Dan Rutherford has used copper and glass in a vertical water feature to add extra warmth and vigour to this small courtyard at night.

25 Vladimir Sitta plays with fire for maximum effect in this inspired design for a small courtyard.

26 Gregor Kregar's three-dimensional work *Polyhedron construction 1*, from Sculpture OnShore, 2006, is lit from within at night.

27 With its warmly glowing pools of light, this arrangement by Alexander McClew at the Ellerslie Flower Show, 2007, captures the feeling of a balmy tropical evening.

28 Philip Nash won gold with this garden at Chelsea in 2004. Transformed by soft aqua lighting in the evening, an elevated steel-edged terrace reached by a glass walkway appears to almost float on the water.

smoother finish. However, the latter is far more challenging as you place the pieces front down so you can't see the pattern developing.

It is often the slight imperfections that give crafted artefacts their charm. Hand-thrown pots that show evidence of the process and the potter's touch have vastly more appeal than those mass-produced in a factory. So too with pebble mosaics. These can now be designed by computers and the resulting pieces are perfect, with every pebble matching its neighbour exactly, but somehow they have lost that special factor of human imperfection – our awareness and appreciation of painstaking work by a skilled craftsperson practising an ancient art.

Grottoes or embellished caves are another ancient art-form that is being rediscovered and reinvented by craft enthusiasts. The principles are the same as those used in mosaic decoration, except that you apply sea shells or bits of glass, polished by the ocean, instead of tiles and broken china. A tapestry effect is created by making blocks of coloured texture of one type of shell, alternating with others in a

27. Pools of light.	**28.** Steel and Glass.

29 Water trickles down over mosaic balls rising above the water lily pads in the Glendowie garden of mosaic artist Sally Lornie. The pattern on the trough reflects the view of Brown's Island and the swirling waves of the sea. Teapot lids and cup handles add extra texture.

30 A bright blue mosaic ball by Kevin Kilsby draws the eye towards a contrasting, colourful mass of bromeliads and a cycad in his own garden.

31 Nestled among fleshy green foliage plants, this cheerful lizard by Sue Booth adds focus and awareness.

32 Intricately decorated mosaic poles by Geoff Dixon are a feature of Frank and Vicki Boffa's garden in Waikanae.

33 Originally created by Margot Knox, this iconic garden in Hawthorn, Melbourne, shows what mosaic can achieve in the hands of a skilled artist with vision.

34 Kevin Kilsby captures the innately appealing shape of the koru, or curled fern frond, in this gathering of the species.

pre-determined pattern, until you have covered the whole area. More than a simple mirror frame or decorated container, the resulting follies make fascinating garden features. They no longer need to be full-sized caves, complete with eerily dripping water, but can metamorphose into shell-covered walls, pillars, water features or pieces of sculpture – whatever takes your fancy.

If you enjoyed unravelling mazes in your childhood puzzle books but thought that they belonged solely in enormous country estates belonging to the local castle or manor house, think again. Dating back to the ancient Egyptians, they too are on the come-back trail, having never really disappeared as there have always been people held fast in their addictive grip. Clever gardeners can insert mazes in

29. Mosaic water feature.

30. Mosaic ball.

31. Tuatara.

32. Mosaic poles.

33. Mosaic garden.

34. Fern fronds.

35. Adam and Eve.

35 Artist Josie Martin has created an organic, colourful and altogether magical garden, with inspiration from Gaudi, at her home, THE GIANT'S HOUSE, in Akaroa. The figures of Adam and Eve capture the imagination of visitors, who enjoy imitating the poses for photographs.

36 Leading up past the sentinel angels to a major staircase, this pathway shows the attention to detail in each and every part of the garden.

37 Symbolic of Josie's spiritually uplifting and joyous garden, The Angel and Magician look down over their domain.

a tiny front garden – a fresh take on the knot garden. The key is a simple pattern on the ground plane; not necessarily 3 m high hedges to make sure you get disoriented and lose your way. It would be fun to include one in a paved courtyard or even on a lawn, where you could have a low hedge or a narrow line marking out the pattern in brick or stone. As with a labyrinth deep under the ground, you can insert dead ends, blocked ways and trails leading nowhere, with only one true path leading to the centre: the core of being. The difference is that your maze will be open to view, and a highly attractive addition to the garden.

36. Pathway.

37. The Angel and Magician.

38 Visitors can sit and linger in this private spot, The Wood Pigeon Mirror House, enjoying the vignettes of the garden reflected in the mirror mosaics on the inside of the walls.

39 Mosaic acrobats balancing balls enliven a wall covered in light-coloured pieces of china at The Giant's House.

40 A gathering place for friends to sit and relax in the sun around a gentle bubble fountain is overlooked by a personified larger-than-life cat and dog, epitomising the quirky nature of Josie Martin's mosaic wizardry.

Some sculpture works on the premise of illusion or masked reality, so that it looks like something completely different if viewed from a different angle or perspective. The use of letters that can be read both ways, and word sequences that progress from one word through a series of others, changing a single letter each time until they end up with quite another word, are further examples of artistic sleight of hand.

Large land sculptures, or 'land art', can be used to illustrate complex ideas and scientific models, combining skilled design with the search for universal truth. Their size and altered perspective make us question perceived reality, as it takes on a surreal, almost hallucinatory appearance.

The traditional art of illusion is not lost to gardens of the twenty-first century. It is in the dynamic process of being rediscovered, reborn and reinvented, and clever gardeners will continue to use it to best advantage, to confuse, trick, delight and amuse us with their down-to-earth, yet strangely ethereal wit and wisdom.

38. The Wood Pigeon Mirror House.

39. The Hot Potato Troupe.

Acknowledgements

We would like to thank all the garden owners who made this book possible by kindly allowing us to photograph their inspirational gardens. We also owe a vote of thanks to Barbara Nielsen of Stylus Publishing Services for the original idea and title of this book, way back in 2001. Fiona Lascelles has done wonders with the design, keeping a cool head when faced with a mountain of photographic material. The team at Random House have been unfailing in their support, especially Nicola Legat, Claire Gummer, Kate Barraclough and Sam Hill.

l = left, c = centre, r = right, d = design, o = owner/s, s = sculptor, a = artist, mos. a = mosaic artist, p = potter, arch. = architect/s, eng. = engineer, orig. d = original designer

Contents

p3 l s Dan Rutherford, Christchurch; c Papudo Garden, Chile, d Juan Grimm; r o/d Made Wijaya, Sanur, Bali.

Introduction

p4 s Rick Rudd, Wanganui. **p5** o/d Russell Fransham, Matapouri Bay. **p6** Papudo Garden, Chile, d Juan Grimm. **p7** l o/d Kevin Kilsby; r o/d Fiona Brockhoff, Karkalla, Victoria, Australia. **p8** l s Tui Hobson, o Nora West, Ponsonby, Auckland; r o/d Matt Wilson, Wellington. **p9** glass a James McMurtrie, d John Middleton, Melbourne International Flower and Garden Show, 2006.

Welcome

p11 1. & **p12** 2. d Mark Read, Natural Habitats, Auckland. **p13** 3. d Trish Bartlett; 4. gate d Noel Gregg, d Jeremy Head, o Gerard Smyth. **p14** 5. orig. d William Kent, Rousham House, Oxfordshire, UK. **p16** 10. o/d Elizabeth Baird, Auckland; 11. o/d Anne Coney, gate d Noel Gregg. **p17** 12. & 13. o/d Sally Lyttleton. **p18** 16. o Ruth and Don Simons, Auckland. **p19** 17. o/d Emma and Stephen Plowright, Glen Iris, Melbourne. **p20** 18. d Mark Read, Natural Habitats, Auckland. **p21** 20. s Marté Szirmay; 22. d Malcolm Talyor. **p23** 24. d Out from the Blue, Melbourne; 25. d Xanthe White, Ellerslie Flower Show, 2004. **p24** 26. d Trudy Crerar; 27. o/d Juan Grimm, Bahia Azul, Los Vilos, Chile. **p25** 28. d Isabelle Greene, Santa Barbara, California, US. **p26** 29. d Juan Grimm, arch. Borja Huidobro, Papudo Garden, Papudo, Chile. **p27** 30. o/d Glynn Williams. **p28** 32. d Richard Matthews and Seng Cheah, Waimauku, Auckland; 35. gate d Jeff Thomson, o/d Kevin Kilsby; 36. o/d Thomas Hobbs, Vancouver, British Columbia, Canada. **p29** 37. d Maureen Busby, Chelsea Flower show, 2004. **p30** 38. d Robin Shafer, Auckland, o Heather and Philip Skelton, St Heliers, Auckland. **p31** 40. o/d Leila and Angus MacDonald. **p32** 41. a Dick Frizzell. **p33** 43. o/d Rebecca Wilson, Eastbourne, Wellington. **p34** 44. s Tim Holman, Coromandel; 45. o/d Matt Wilson, Wellington; 46. gate d Dave Vazey, o Glenn Crewther and Bruce Fraser, Glendowie, Auckland. **p35** 47. s Chris Booth, Takahanga Marae, Kaikoura.

Walls

p37 1. Ibah Hotel, Ubud, Bali. **p38** 2. d Nigel Cameron, Auckland; 3. o/d Sally and John Woodham, Haumoana, Hawke's Bay; 4. Royal Botanic Gardens, Sydney. **p40** 5. d Richard Unsworth, Garden Life, Sydney. **p41** 6. d Susan Firth, Auckland; 7. d Vladimir Sitta, Sydney. **p42** 8. Ibah Hotel, Ubud, Bali. **p43** 9. o/d Liz Morrow, Parnell, Auckland; 10. & 11. d Vladimir Sitta, Sydney. **p44** 12. d Sue McLean, o Ann and Neville Hay, Alfriston, Auckland. **p45** 13. d Eckersley Stafford Design, Melbourne; 14. d Cilla Cooper, Takapuna. **p46** 15. d Vladimir Sitta, Sydney. **p47** 16. d Marion Morris, Fendalton, Christchurch; 17, Hidcote Manor Garden, Cotswold, UK; 18. d Kim Jarrett, Wellington. **p48** 19. o/d Michael Trapp, Connecticut, US. **p49** 20. d Rebecca Wilson, Eastbourne, Wellington; 22. s Walter Bailey, Hannah Perchar Sculpture Garden, Surrey, UK. **p50** 23. arch & d E'xtra Paysage, Italy, Chaumont-sur-Loire Garden Festival, France, 2006. **p51** 24. d Jeremy Head, o Gerard Smyth, Christchurch; 25. d Arpents Paysages, France, Chaumont, 2006. **p52** 26. d Giardino sonoro & arch nEmoGruppo architects, Italy, Chaumont, 2006; 27. Chinese Garden of Friendship, Darling Harbour, Sydney. **p53** 28. d Sandra Arnet, Ellerslie Flower Show. **p54** 29. Chaumont-sur-Loire Garden Festival, 2006. **p55** 30. d NB architectes, France, Chaumont, 2006; 31. s Walter Bailey, Hannah Peschar Sculpture Garden, Surrey, UK. **p56** 32. o/d Ron Sang and Margaret Parker, Auckland; 33. d Ted Smyth, Auckland. **p57** 34. d Norma de Langen, lighting d Jenny Pullar, Ellerslie, 2005.

Ground

p59 1. o/d Richard Matthews and Seng Cheah, Waimauku, Auckland. **p60** 2. d Trish Bartlett, o Andrew Bowker and Janet Rowan; 3. o/s Rick Rudd, Castlecliff, Wanganui. **p61** 4. d Leo Jew, o Paul Holmes and Deborah Hamilton Holmes. **p62** 5. d Lucy Treep, o Rose Thodey; 6. d Trish Bartlett, o Peter and Sally Jackson; 7. o/d Marion Morris, Fendalton, Christchurch. **p63** 8. d Philip Stray, Crafted Landscapes, Melbourne. 9. d Juan Grimm, Chiñihue Garden, Melipilla, Chile. **p64** 10. o/d David Brundell, Gardenza, Glenbrook, Auckland. **p65** 11. Bloedel Reserve, Bainbridge Island, Washington, US; 12. o/d Jeff and Shelley Peet. **p66** 13. d Josie Martin, The Giant's House, Akaroa; 14. o/d Elaine and John Lynn, Millstream Garden, Ohoka, North Canterbury. **p67** 15. d Made Wijaya, Tirtha Uluwata, Bali. **p68** 16. d Anthony Paul, Hannah Peschar Sculpture Garden, Surrey, UK. **p69** 17. d Alex Schanzer, Ellerslie, 2004; 18. d Ian Fryer, Christchurch. **p70** 19. d Isabelle Greene, California, US; 20. s John Edgar, o/d John Edgar and Ann Robinson, Karekare, Auckland. **p71** 21. d Vladimir Sitta, Sydney. **p73** 22. d Isabelle Greene, California, US; 23. d Peter Nixon, Paradisus Garden Design, Sydney; 24. d Vladimir Sitta, Sydney. **p74** 25. Chinese Scholar's Garden, Hamilton Gardens; 26. d Philip Stray, Crafted Landscapes, Melbourne; 27. Graham Cleary, Natural Habitats, Auckland; 28. Peter Nixon, Paradisus, Sydney; 29. pebble mos. a Mark Davidson, Morrinsville. **p75** 30. o/d Philip Stray, Crafted Landscapes, Melbourne. 31. d Craig Smith, Pershore College, Chelsea Flower Show, 2004. **p77** 32. o/d Anne Coney, Parnell, Auckland; 33. d Rebecca Wilson, Earthwork Landscape Architects, Wellington; 34. o/d Kevin Kilsby, Mt Albert, Auckland. **p78** 35. Lotusland, near Santa Barbara, California, US. **p79** 36. d Dimitri Xenakis and Maro Avrabou, France-Greece, Chaumont, 2006.

Living

p81 1. a Céline Dodelin, eng d Matthieu Lanher & d François Wattellier, France, Chaumont-sur-Loire Garden Festival, France, 2006. **p82** 2.& 4. o/d Vivien Papich, Bellevue, Langs Beach; 3. o/d Made Wijaya, Sanur, Bali. **p83** 5. o/d Vivien Papich, Bellevue, Langs Beach. **p84** 6. d Nancy McCabe, Connecticut, US; 7. o/d Jo Wallis, Mt Baku Downs, Wanaka; 8. o/d Vivien Papich, Bellevue, Langs Beach; 9. s Alison Crowther, Hannah Peschar Sculpture Garden, Surrey, UK; 10. o/d Mr. Patricio Cummins, Quinta Nicolasa, Las Condes, Santiago, Chile; 11. d Vladimir Sitta, Sydney; 13. o/d Vivien Papich, Langs Beach. **p85** 14. d Emmeline Johnston & Chris Bourne, Chelsea Flower Show, 2004. **p86** 15. o/d Juan Grimm, Bahia Azul, Los Vilos, Chile. **p87** 18. d Juan Grimm, Chiñihue Garden, Melipilla, Chile. **p88** 19. d Matt McIsaac and Mat Ransom, Watch this Space Landscapes, Ellerslie Flower Show, 2007; 20. d Chris Goom, Christchurch. **p89** 21. d Cilla Cooper. **p90** 22. d Hadrian Whittle, Hampton Court Palace Flower Show, 2006. **p91** 23. and 25. o/d Rae Jones-Evans Landscape Design, Melbourne; 24. d Jim Fogarty Design, Melbourne. **p93** 27. d Brent Reid, Melbourne International Flower and Garden Show, 2006. **p94** 28. arch. Pip Cheshire and Malcolm Taylor. **p95** 29. d Georgina Martyn, Bold Simplicity, Melbourne; 30. d Kirsten Sach, Jamie Douglas and Zoë Carafice, Ellerslie Flower Show, 2007. **p96** 31. d Vladimir Sitta. **p97** 32. d Yano Tea, Chelsea Flower Show, 2004; 33. d Alison Sloga, Hampton Court Place Flower Show, 2006. **p98** 34. d Juan Grimm, Chiñihue Garden, Melipilla, Chile; 35. o/d Richard Matthews and Seng Cheah, Waimauku, Auckland. **p99** 36. Chaumont-sur-Loire Garden Festival, 2006. **p101** 38. The Mosaic Garden, Hawthorn, Melbourne; 39. o/d Elaine and John Lynn, Millstream Garden, Ohoka, North Canterbury; 40. d Chris Goom, o Viv and Mike Pooley, Motunau, North Canterbury. **p102** 41. d Ben McMaster, Christchurch; 42. o/d Anne Coney, Parnell, Auckland. **p103** 43. d Gudrun Fischer, o Graeme and Robyn Hart, Auckland. **p104** 44. o/d Elaine and John Lynn, Millstream Garden, Ohoka, North Canterbury. **p105** 45. o Peter and Annie Webb; 46. d Trish Bartlett, o Dona and Gavin White, Freemans Bay, Auckland. **p106** 47. o/d Sally and John Woodham, Haumoana, Hawke's Bay; 48. o/d Jerry Tressler and Annie Ulyate. **p107** 49. o/d John and Maxine Lees, Auckland.

Sculpture

p109 1. s Gary Baynes, Sculpture OnShore, 2004, Fort Takapuna Historic Reserve, Auckland. **p110** 2. s Paul Millin, Rannoch, James Wallace Arts Trust, Auckland. **p111** 3. s Paul Dibble, Ravenscar Garden, Taylor's Mistake, Christchurch; 4. s Paul Dibble, Sculpture in the Gardens, Auckland Botanic Gardens, 2007-2008. **p112** 5. s Bronwynne Cornish. **p113** 6. s David McCracken, o Tom Mutch, Coromandel; 7. s Helen Pollock, Sculpture OnShore, Becroft Garden, Takapuna, 1998; 8. s Terry Stringer, o Frank and Vicki Boffa, Waikanae. **p114** 9. s Patricia Volk, Hannah Peschar Sculpture Garden, Surrey, UK. **p115** 10. s Patricia Volk, Hannah Peschar Sculpture Garden, Surrey, UK; 11. s Terry Stringer, Zealandia, Mahurangi West, Warkworth. **p116** 12. s Meryn Saccente, Auckland; 13. s Arnold Wilson, Auckland; 14. s Para Matchitt, Ellerslie Flower Show, 2005. **p117** 15. s Para Matchitt, Ellerslie Flower Show, 2005. **p118** 16. s Jeff Thomson, Brick Bay Sculpture Trail, Warkworth. **p119** 17. d Jenny Smith Gardens, Melbourne; 18. s Jeff Thomson, Waiheke Island. **p120** 19. s Virginia King, o Andrew Bowker and Janet Rowan, Auckland. **p121** 20. s Neil Dawson, Sculpture OnShore, Becroft Garden, Takapuna; 21. s Virginia King, Sculpture in the Gardens,

Castlecliff, Wanganui; 17. d Nancy McCabe, Connecticut, US. **p249** 18. o/s Rick Rudd, Castlecliff, Wanganui. **p250** 19–26. o/s Rick Rudd, Castlecliff, Wanganui. **p251** 27. o/s Rick Rudd, Castlecliff, Wanganui. **p252** 28. & 29. d Juan Grimm, Chiñihue Garden, Melipilla, Chile.**p253** 30. o/s Rick Rudd, Castlecliff, Wanganui. **p254** 31. o/d Ivan Hicks, UK; 32. o/d Jeff and Tatti Howarth, Waiau Waterworks, Coromandel. **p255** 34. o/d Ivan Hicks, UK; 35. o/d Jeff and Tatti Howarth, Waiau Waterworks, Coromandel. **p256** 38. o/d Christine and Tony Peek, Woodbridge, Coatesville. **p257** 41. orig. o/d Clark Abbott, Greagh, Whangarei. **p258** 42. mos. a/d Kevin Kilsby, Mt Albert, Auckland; 43. s Jeff Thomson, Becroft Garden, Takapuna. **p259** 44. Whitley, Southern Highlands, NSW. **p260** 45. s Jeff Thomson, Rannoch, James Wallace Arts Trust, Auckland. **p261** 46. s Jeff Thomson, o David and Gail Nathan, Auckland; 47. o/d Susanna and Christopher Grace, Rathmoy, Hunterville.

Illusion

p263 1. s Allan Coleman, Sculpture OnShore, 2006.
p264 2. d Cilla Cooper. **p265** 3. o/d Heather Swinburn; 4. o/d Graeme Ross, Beach Haven, Auckland. **p266** 5. d Microclimax: Benjamin Jacquemet & Carolyn Wittendal, France, Chaumont-sur-Loire Festival, 2006; 6. d Maria-Josefina Casares, Martina Barzi, Maria Noël, Tomas Camps & Damian Ayarza, Argentina. Chaumont-sur-Loire Garden Festival, 2006, France. **p267** 7. o/d Dennis Greville, Christchurch. **p268** 8. d Sayburn Miller, Auckland. **p269** 9. a Jane Watt, Westonbirt Arboretum Festival, Gloucestershire, 2004; 10. d Trish Bartleet, o Margot Edwards and Dave Milne, Auckland. **p270** 11. o/d Louise Goldsack, Karori, Wellington; 12. d Lesley Kennedy, Westonbirt Arboretum Festival, Gloucestershire, 2004. **p271** 13. s Gregor Kregar, Brick Bay Sculpture Trail, Warkworth. **p272** 14. d Out from the Blue, Melbourne. **p273** 15. a Melissa Langford, d Eckersley Stafford Design, Melbourne; 16. d Anne Thomson, Sydney. **p274** 17. s Terry Stringer, Zealandia, Mahurangi West, Warkworth; 18. s Neil Dawson, o/d Sir Miles Warren, Ohinetahi, Governor's Bay, Canterbury. **p275** 19. s Terry Stringer, arch. Pip Cheshire, Zealandia, Mahurangi West, Warkworth. **p276** 20. orig. o/d Frank and Anne Cabot, Stonecrop Gardens, Cold Spring, New York. **p277** 21. o/d Richard and Susan MacFarlane, Winterhome, Marlborough; 22. Chinese Garden of Friendship, Darling Harbour, Sydney 23. d Richard Greenwood, Ellerslie Flower Show. **p278** 24. d Dan Rutherford, Christchurch; 25. d Vladimir Sitta, Sydney; 26. s Gregor Kregar, Sculpture OnShore, 2006. **p279** 27. d Alexander McClew, Ellerslie Flower Show, 2007; 28. d Philip Nash, Chelsea Flower Show, 2004. **p280** 29. mos. a/o Sally Lornie, Glendowie, Auckland. **p281** 30. mos. a/o Kevin Kilsby, Mt Albert, Auckland; 31. mos. a Sue Booth, o/d Landsendt, Oratia, Auckland; 32. mos. a Geoff Dixon, o/d Frank and Vicki Boffa, Waikanae; 33. The Mosaic Garden, Hawthorn, Melbourne; 34. mos. a/o Kevin Kilsby, Mt Albert, Auckland. **p282–85** 35–40. mos. a Josie Martin, The Giant's House, Akaroa, Canterbury.

Rose Thodey has been a gardening writer for over 20 years, writing principally for the *New Zealand Herald* and *New Zealand Gardener* magazine before being appointed Gardens Editor of *New Zealand House & Garden* in 2008. A former Ellerslie Flower Show judge, she is the author of several books, including *Gardening with Old Roses* (with Alan Sinclair), *Floranova* (with Warwick Orme) and, with Gil Hanly, *Landscape: Gardens by New Zealand's Top Designers*, published by Godwit in 2005.

Gil Hanly has been a photographer for over 25 years. Focussing initially on social, political and environmental issues, she has concentrated on garden photography over the last 12 years and her work appears widely in both books and magazines. She has been the photographer for 15 gardening books.

A GODWIT book published by Random House New Zealand
18 Poland Road, Glenfield, Auckland, New Zealand

For more information about our titles go to www.randomhouse.co.nz

A catalogue record for this book is available from the National Library of New Zealand

Random House International, Random House, 20 Vauxhall Bridge Road, London, SW1V 2SA, United Kingdom; **Random House Australia Pty Ltd**, Level 3, 100 Pacific Highway, North Sydney 2060, Australia; **Random House South Africa Pty Ltd**, Isle of Houghton, Corner Boundary Road and Carse O'Gowrie, Houghton 2198, South Africa; **Random House Publishers India Private Ltd**, 301 World Trade Tower, Hotel Intercontinental Grand Complex, Barakhamba Lane, New Delhi 110 001, India

First published 2008

ISBN 978 1 86962 121 6

Front cover: p236. Back cover (clockwise from top left): p181, 125, 124, 37, 28, 14, 148, 170.

Design: Fiona Lascelles
Printed in China by Everbest Printing Co Ltd